First World War
and Army of Occupation
War Diary
France, Belgium and Germany

55 DIVISION
165 Infantry Brigade
King's (Liverpool Regiment)
9th Battalion
1 January 1916 - 28 February 1919

WO95/2927/2

The Naval & Military Press Ltd
www.nmarchive.com
Published in association with The National Archives

Published by

The Naval & Military Press Ltd

Unit 10 Ridgewood Industrial Park,

Uckfield, East Sussex,

TN22 5QE England

Tel: +44 (0) 1825 749494

www.naval-military-press.com

www.nmarchive.com

This diary has been reprinted in facsimile from the original. Any imperfections are inevitably reproduced and the quality may fall short of modern type and cartographic standards.

© Crown Copyright

Images reproduced by permission of The National Archives, London, England, 2015.

Contents

Document type	Place/Title	Date From	Date To
Heading	1/9th King's Liverpool		
Miscellaneous	55th Division 165th Infy Bde 1-9th King's Liverpool Regt Jan 1916-Jan 1918 From 1 Div 2 Bde To 57 Div 172 Bde		
War Diary	G23 And G24	01/01/1916	01/01/1916
War Diary	H 25 A To H 19 A	02/01/1916	04/01/1916
War Diary	G23 And G24	05/01/1916	05/01/1916
War Diary	Philosophe	06/01/1916	07/01/1916
War Diary	Hocquincourt	08/01/1916	20/01/1916
War Diary	Merelessart	21/01/1916	06/02/1916
War Diary	Longpres	07/02/1916	07/02/1916
War Diary	Berteaucourt	09/02/1916	13/02/1916
War Diary	Berles-Au-Bois Monchiet	15/02/1916	15/02/1916
War Diary	Wailly	16/02/1916	07/04/1916
War Diary	Beaumetz Les-Loges	08/04/1916	13/04/1916
War Diary	Wailly	14/04/1916	30/04/1916
War Diary	Wailly Trenches Beaumetz	01/05/1916	08/05/1916
War Diary	Wailly	09/05/1916	28/05/1916
War Diary	Beaumetz	29/05/1916	02/06/1916
War Diary	Wailly Sector	03/06/1916	11/06/1916
War Diary	Wailly Village	12/06/1916	26/06/1916
War Diary	Wailly Trenches	27/06/1916	30/06/1916
Heading	165th Brigade. 55th Division 1/9th Battalion The King's Liverpool Regiment July 1916		
Heading	War Diary Of The 1/9th Liverpool Regt. 165th Infantry Brigade 55th (West Lancashire) Division For The Period 1st July 1916 To 31st July 1916. Vol 15		
War Diary	Wailly Trenches	01/07/1916	08/07/1916
War Diary	Gouy	09/07/1916	19/07/1916
War Diary	Sus-St-Leger	20/07/1916	20/07/1916
War Diary	Halloy	21/07/1916	21/07/1916
War Diary	Autheux	22/07/1916	25/07/1916
War Diary	Mericourt	26/07/1916	28/07/1916
War Diary	K 17 B7 K11d	29/07/1916	30/07/1916
War Diary	F 14 D & F 20A	31/07/1916	31/07/1916
Heading	165th Brigade 55th Division. 1/9th Battalion The King's Liverpool Regiment August 1916		
War Diary	Bivouac Area F 20 B F23 A	01/08/1916	03/08/1916
War Diary	Trones Wood Sector	04/08/1916	07/08/1916
War Diary	Talus Boise A9.c.9.6	08/08/1916	11/08/1916
War Diary	Maltz Horn Farm Area	12/08/1916	14/08/1916
War Diary	F2 3A Ville-Sur-Ancre	14/08/1916	19/08/1916
War Diary	Ramburelle	20/08/1916	31/08/1916
Miscellaneous	9th King's (Liverpool Regiment)	21/08/1916	21/08/1916
Heading	War Diary Of 1/9th Kings Liverpool Regt. 1st September To 30th September 1916		
War Diary	Dernacourt	01/09/1916	04/09/1916
War Diary	Montauban Alley Reserve Trenches	04/09/1916	07/09/1916
War Diary	Tea Trench	07/09/1916	10/09/1916
War Diary	F13a	11/09/1916	11/09/1916

War Diary	Buire	12/09/1916	16/09/1916
War Diary	E 14 D	17/09/1916	17/09/1916
War Diary	Flers Trenches	18/09/1916	18/09/1916
War Diary	York Trench	19/09/1916	19/09/1916
War Diary	Pommier Redoubt	20/09/1916	23/09/1916
War Diary	Flers Trench	24/09/1916	26/09/1916
War Diary	York	27/09/1916	27/09/1916
War Diary	Trench	27/09/1916	27/09/1916
War Diary	Buire Sur Ancre	28/09/1916	29/09/1916
Heading	War Diary Of 1/9th Liverpool Regiment For The Period 1st To 31st October 1916		
War Diary	Buire	01/10/1916	01/10/1916
War Diary	Cocqueril	02/10/1916	02/10/1916
War Diary	Wormhoudt	03/10/1916	04/10/1916
War Diary	Ypres	05/10/1916	05/10/1916
War Diary	Ypres Trenches	06/10/1916	06/10/1916
War Diary	Ypres Trenches (Railway Wood Sector)	07/10/1916	10/10/1916
War Diary	Ypres	11/10/1916	14/10/1916
War Diary	Elverdinghe	15/10/1916	22/10/1916
War Diary	Elverdinghe and Ypres	22/10/1916	22/10/1916
War Diary	Ypres and Ypres Trenches	23/10/1916	23/10/1916
War Diary	Ypres Trenches (Railway Wood Sector)	24/10/1916	26/10/1916
War Diary	Ypres	27/10/1916	31/10/1916
Heading	War Diary Of 1/9th Liverpool Regt For Period Of 1st November To 30th November 1916		
War Diary	Potijze Ypres (Trenches)	01/11/1916	04/11/1916
War Diary	Ypres	05/11/1916	07/11/1916
War Diary	B Camp G B.d.4.2.	08/11/1916	18/11/1916
War Diary	Ypres	19/11/1916	30/11/1916
Heading	War Diary Of 1/9th Liverpool, Regt. For Period December 1st-31st 1916		
War Diary	Ypres	01/12/1916	12/12/1916
War Diary	B Camp	13/12/1916	17/12/1916
War Diary	Ypres	18/12/1916	31/12/1916
Heading	War Diary Of The 1/9th Liverpool R For The Period 1/1/17 To 31/1/17.		
War Diary	Ypres	01/01/1917	13/01/1917
War Diary	Z Camp (St. Jahn-Ter-Biezen)	14/01/1917	28/01/1917
War Diary	Z Camp St. Jan-Ter-Biezen and Proven	29/01/1917	29/01/1917
War Diary	Proven	30/01/1917	31/01/1917
Heading	War Diary Of 1/9th Liverpool Regt For The Period 1st To 28th February 1917		
War Diary	Proven	01/02/1917	22/02/1917
War Diary	Proven And Ypres	23/02/1917	23/02/1917
War Diary	Ypres Railway Wood Sector	24/02/1917	28/02/1917
Heading	War Diary Of The 1/9 Liverpool R for the Period 1st To 31st March 1917		
War Diary	Ypres Railway Wood Sector	01/03/1917	03/03/1917
War Diary	Ypres	03/03/1917	06/03/1917
War Diary	Brandhoek "C" Camp	07/03/1917	16/03/1917
War Diary	Ypres	17/03/1917	17/03/1917
War Diary	Ypres Railway Wood Sector	18/03/1917	21/03/1917
War Diary	Ypres	22/03/1917	26/03/1917
War Diary	Railway Wood Sector	27/03/1917	28/03/1917
War Diary	Ypres Railway Wood Sector	29/03/1917	31/03/1917

Heading	War Diary Of 1/9 Liverpool R For The Period 1st April To 30th April 1917		
Miscellaneous	55th Division.	02/04/1917	02/04/1917
War Diary	Railway Wood Sector Ypres	01/04/1917	01/04/1917
War Diary	Ypres	02/04/1917	06/04/1917
War Diary	C Camp	07/04/1917	18/04/1917
War Diary	Ecole Ypres	18/04/1917	23/04/1917
War Diary	Railway Wood Sector	24/04/1917	29/04/1917
War Diary	C Camp	30/04/1917	30/04/1917
Heading	War Diary Of 1/9th Liverpool R For The Period May 1st To 31st, 1917 Vol 25		
War Diary	C.Camp	01/05/1917	11/05/1917
War Diary	Railway Wood Sector	06/05/1917	11/05/1917
War Diary	Ecole	12/05/1917	16/05/1917
War Diary	B Camp	17/05/1917	17/05/1917
War Diary	Bollezeele	17/05/1917	31/05/1917
Heading	War Diary Of 1/9th Liverpool R For The Period June 1st To June 30th 1917		
War Diary	Bollezeele	01/06/1917	12/06/1917
War Diary	Potijze Sector	12/06/1917	15/06/1917
War Diary	Wieltje Sector	15/06/1917	30/06/1917
Heading	War Diary Of The 1/9 Liverpool R For The Period 1st July To 31st July 1917		
War Diary	Wieltje	01/07/1917	03/07/1917
War Diary	Query Camp	03/07/1917	03/07/1917
War Diary	Boisdinghem	03/07/1917	06/07/1917
War Diary	Moringhem	06/07/1917	21/07/1917
War Diary	B Camp	21/07/1917	29/07/1917
War Diary	Durham Redoubt	30/07/1917	30/07/1917
War Diary	Oxford Trench	31/07/1917	31/07/1917
Heading	War Diary Of 1/9th Liverpool R For Period 1st To 31st August 1917		
War Diary	Oxford Trench	31/07/1917	03/08/1917
War Diary	Vlamertinghe	03/08/1917	04/08/1917
War Diary	Abeele	04/08/1917	06/08/1917
War Diary	Blanc Pignon	06/08/1917	30/08/1917
Heading	War Diary Of 1/9 Liverpool R For Period 1/9/17-30/9/17		
War Diary	Blanc Pignon	01/09/1917	15/09/1917
War Diary	Vlamertinghe	15/09/1917	25/09/1917
War Diary	Bapaume	26/09/1917	26/09/1917
War Diary	Barastre Area	26/09/1917	30/09/1917
Miscellaneous	55th (West Lancashire) Division Order Of The Day.	23/09/1917	23/09/1917
Miscellaneous	55th (West Lancashire) Division Order Of The Day.	22/09/1917	22/09/1917
Miscellaneous	55th (West Lancashire) Division Order Of The Day.	21/09/1917	21/09/1917
Miscellaneous	55th (West Lancashire) Division Order Of The Day.	24/09/1917	24/09/1917
Heading	War Diary Of 1/9th Liverpool R For The Period 1st To 31st October 1917		
War Diary	Aizecourt-Le-Bas	01/10/1917	01/10/1917
War Diary	St Emilie	02/10/1917	06/10/1917
War Diary	Lempire	07/10/1917	12/10/1917
War Diary	Adelphi	12/10/1917	18/10/1917
War Diary	Vaughans Bank	18/10/1917	22/10/1917
War Diary	Hamel	22/10/1917	31/10/1917
Heading	War Diary Of The 1/9th Liverpool For The Period 1st To 30th November 1917		

Heading	55 Div A.Q Herewith War Diary 9 K.L.R Up to the time of Leaving the Division		
War Diary		01/11/1918	30/11/1918
War Diary	Guillemont Farm	30/11/1918	30/11/1918
Heading	War Diary Of The 1/9th Liverpool R For The Period 1st To 31st December 1917.		
War Diary	Lempire	01/12/1917	05/12/1917
War Diary	St Emelie	06/12/1917	06/12/1917
War Diary	Peronne	06/12/1917	08/12/1917
War Diary	Moreuille	10/12/1917	10/12/1917
War Diary	Bailluie	12/12/1917	12/12/1917
War Diary	E.P.S.	13/12/1917	13/12/1917
War Diary	Lisbourg	15/12/1917	31/01/1918
War Diary	Uccle	01/02/1919	28/02/1919

1/9th
King's Liverpool

55TH DIVISION
165TH INFY BDE

1-9TH KING'S LIVERPOOL REGT

JAN 1916-JAN 1918

FROM 1 DIV.
2 Bde

TO 57 DIV
172 Bde

Army Form C. 2118.

WAR DIARY
or
INTELLIGENCE SUMMARY. — 9th Bn. The KING'S (LIVERPOOL REGT.)
(Erase heading not required.)

Instructions regarding War Diaries and Intelligence Summaries are contained in F. S. Regs., Part II. and the Staff Manual respectively. Title pages will be prepared in manuscript.

Hour, Date, Place	Summary of Events and Information	Remarks and references to Appendices
1916		
January 1 G23 and G24	In reserve trenches. One other rank wounded.	TRENCH MAP 36c NW.3 and parts of 1, 2 and 4 and BETHUNE COMBINED SHEET
5 pm	Moved into front line trenches from H25A85 to H19A08 and took over from 6th WELCH. 1st GLOUCESTERS on right.	
7 pm	1st BLACK WATCH on left. 4 platoons of 9th ROYAL DUBLIN FUSILIERS attached for instruction.	
2 H25A & H19A	Improvement and repair of trenches. Germans shelled front and support lines rather heavily with heavy and field guns. No great harm done. Our artillery replied. Weather fine till evening. Wet night. One other rank killed and five wounded.	
10 am to 4 pm		
3	Fine day. German guns more active than usual. Ours retaliate.	
4	Same as 3rd. One officer Lt W.R. PERRY wounded.	

Army Form C. 2118.

9th Bn. The KING'S
(LIVERPOOL REGT.)

WAR DIARY
— or —
INTELLIGENCE SUMMARY.
(*Erase heading not required.*)

Hour, Date, Place	Summary of Events and Information	Remarks and references to Appendices
1916		
January 4. 6.30 pm	Relieved by 6th WELCH. Handed over detachment of ROYAL DUBLIN FUSILIERS in G23 and G24 to them and returned to reserve.	
5. G23 and G24	Fine	
. 7.30 pm	Relieved by 2nd ROYAL SUSSEX in G20 A sov.	
6. PHILOSOPHE	at PHILOSOPHE and marched to billets	
	Resting and cleaning equipment etc. sov.	
7	Battalion left 3rd Brigade	
8 am.	One company	
9 am.	M.G. Section and Transport } left billets and marched to BETHUNE.	
11 am.	Remainder of battalion	
12.30 pm	One company entrained	
3.30 pm.	Remainder entrained. Proceeded by train to PONT REMY and thence (by route march twenty) HOCQUINCOURT 7 miles south of ABBEVILLE.	FRANCE 1/80,000 ABBEVILLE 11

Army Form C. 2118.

WAR DIARY
or
INTELLIGENCE SUMMARY.
(Erase heading not required.)

9th Bn The KING'S (LIVERPOOL REGT.)

Instructions regarding War Diaries and Intelligence Summaries are contained in F.S. Regs. Part II. and the Staff Manual respectively. Title pages will be prepared in manuscript.

Hour, Date, Place	Summary of Events and Information	Remarks and references to Appendices
1916		
January 8 HOCQUINCOURT 10am.	Arrived at HOCQUINCOURT and went into billets. Rest, cleaning etc. Battalion now forms part of 165 Brigade, 55 Division, 14 Corps, III Army. Received draft of 40 other ranks.	
9	Inspection etc.	
10	Inspections and training.	
11	Training.	
12	Training.	
13	Training.	
14	Training.	
15	Training.	
16	Rest.	
17	Training.	
18	Training.	
19	Training.	
20 1.30 pm	Marched to MÉRÉLESSART 2 miles due South of HOCQUINCOURT and went into billets.	

Army Form C. 2118.

WAR DIARY
INTELLIGENCE SUMMARY.
(Erase heading not required.)

9th Bn. The KING'S
(LIVERPOOL REGT.)

Instructions regarding War Diaries and Intelligence Summaries are contained in F.S. Regs., Part II. and the Staff Manual respectively. Title pages will be prepared in manuscript.

Hour, Date, Place	Summary of Events and Information	Remarks and references to Appendices
January 21 MÉRÉLESSART	Training.	
22	Training. Received draft of 2 Officers - 2nd Lt. HARTLEY and 2nd Lt. W.A. REID. and 19 other ranks.	
23	Rest. Lt. Col. F.W. RAMSAY, D.S.O.; relinquished Command of battalion in order to take over command of 48 Infantry Brigade. Captain H.H. COVELL assumed command of battalion.	
24	Training.	
25	Training.	
26	Training.	
27	Training.	
28	Training.	
29	Training.	
30	Rest.	
31	Training.	

H.H. Covell
Capt.
Commanding 9th KING'S

Army Form C. 2118.

WAR DIARY or INTELLIGENCE SUMMARY.

(Erase heading not required.)

1/9th Batt. THE KING'S (Liverpool Regt) T.F.

FEBRUARY 1916

Instructions regarding War Diaries and Intelligence Summaries are contained in F.S. Regs., Part II. and the Staff Manual respectively. Title pages will be prepared in manuscript.

Hour, Date, Place	Summary of Events and Information	Remarks and references to Appendices
1916		
Feb. 2 MERELESSART	Battalion inspected by Lord Derby.	
3 "	Lieut. R.S. WOODWARD, 16th KINGS, posted to this Battalion but attached to 1st Divisional Ammunition Transport in ENGLAND 21-1-16 and struck off strength 3-2-16	Ref Maps SHEET 11 ARRAS VILLE 1:80000
6 (10.0 am) "	Battalion marched to TILLOY then to LONGPRÉS.	" 12 - AMIENS 1:80000
7 (9.0 am) LONGPRÉS	Battalion marched to TOILS to BERTAUCOURT. Capt. & Adjt. C.P.G.R. LEDERER sick in billets.	" 11 - LENS 1:100000
9 BERTAUCOURT	Major C.P. JAMES Acting as Adjutant. Names of Billeting arrived in and afternoon Battalion commanded to billet.	
12 (7.40 am) "	Battalion marched into CANDAS, DULLENS, to stations at AMPLIER. 2/Lieut. L.H. COCKRAM joined in train.	Ref: Maps
13 (10.50 am) "	Battalion moved in THIEVRES, PAS, HENU - ST. AMAND etc. POMMIER to BERLES-AU-BOIS. Transport at POMMIER.	
15 (4.30 am) BERLES-AU-BOIS	Battalion marched into BAILLEULMONT to WAILLY.	FRANCE - SHEET 51C 1:40000
" (4.40 pm) MONCHIET	Battalion marched via BEAUMETZ to WAILLY and attached to supply battalion of the 71st French Regt. A and B Companies but C Company (less 2 platoons) in TERRITORIAL TRENCH, and D Company (less 2 platoons & 1 company on supports)	FICHEUX - 51C SE & 51E SW (sheets) 1:10000
" WAILLY	Capt. C.H. STEWART and 2/Lieut E. JONES joined Battalion. Four LEWIS Guns served to Battalion.	FRENCH MAP
16 "	Relieved 7th KINGS (LIVERPOOL REGT) in M1, M12, M13 and M4. One other name [illegible] (Cairn)	
18 "		
19 "	MAKEUP Sector as Previous.	
23 "	Battalion relieved by 7th KINGS and moved into support at WAILLY	
26 "	2/Lieut F.E. BOUNDY (1st & 2nd KINGS) and three Battalions to whom was attached to join 1/9th KINGS.	
27 "	Relieved 7th KINGS (LIVERPOOL REGT) in lefl half M12, M13, M4.	
28 "	MARBOEUF Sector etc. Major G. BRADLEY BAKOUT arrived & assumed Command Battalion vice Lieut Col. C.P. JAMES.	

(9 29 6) W3332—1107 100,000 10/13 H W V Forms/C. 2118/10.

Army Form C. 2118.

WAR DIARY
or
INTELLIGENCE SUMMARY

(Erase heading not required.)

— APRIL 1916 — 1/5th 1/9th Batt. THE KINGS (Liverpool Regt.) T.F.

Instructions regarding War Diaries and Intelligence Summaries are contained in F.S. Regs., Part II. and the Staff Manual respectively. Title Pages will be prepared in manuscript.

Place	Date	Hour	Summary of Events and Information	Remarks and references to Appendices
WAILLY	1st	3.55pm	The Battalion relieved the 1st KINGS on left front of F sector R.24 C 21 to M 19 V 93. 5 The Battalion on left front A Coy on centre, C Coy on left and B Coy in support. The 6th KINGS on our right and SOMERSETS, 14 Dragoons on our left. Enemy quiet during night. Weather fine.	# FICHEUX &c. 10 O.R.
	2nd	8.45pm	Enemy shelled the SOMERSETS on our left, and then opened rapid fire with machine guns in front of SOMERSETS and our left Coy. Supposed to be enemy raid. 12 minutes bombardment. Enemy were stopped by our rifle fire. Weather fine. Machine guns very active throughout night.	10 O.R.
	3rd		Works: Constructed Sentry Post, traverses & wiring. Enemy very quiet throughout the day.	10 O.R. 10 O.R.
			Our Snipers had good results during the day. Works: Constructing Bombing Posts, wiring into Dugouts. Weather fine.	10 O.R. 10 O.R.
	4th		Enemy active with rifle grenades, otherwise quiet.	10 O.R.
	5th 6th	6.30pm 10.10pm	We observed behind enemy lines. Works: Constructing Bombing Posts & Arms Rest, traverses & Bombing Posts. Weather fine.	10 O.R. 10 O.R.
			The hated sent out by our centre Coy. (Commanding of 1 NCO & 1 man failed to return. They were observed to be carried into German dug-outs only the next morning, both apparently badly wounded.	10 O.R.
	6th		One O.R. accidentally wounded. Weather fine.	
	7th 8th	10.30pm	The Battalion was relieved by 1st KINGS & marched to billets in BEAUMETZ. Weather fine.	10 O.R.
BEAUMETZ LES LOGES			Weather fine. The Battalion found daily working parties of 8 Officers & 193 other ranks. Lieut Cope was Burying Party & Bridgm [?] to Town Major.	10 O.R.
			3 O.R. joined Battalion as reinforcement	
	9th		Col. C.G. BRADLEY D.S.O. & 4 at 2 Lieut J Burn-LE-CHATEAU for Conference. Capt 9.6 LEDERER assumed command. Enemy shelled CHATEAU, wounded two men. Weather fine.	10 F.O. 10 R. 10 R.
			Our D.R. wounded.	
	10th 11th 12th		All available Officers & NCO's flew witnessed a Flammenwerfer demonstration at NONCHIET. Weather fine. Lieuts ROBERTS & 2 O. Ranks proceed to Govy to Divisional School. Weather wet. Battalion was inspected by Brigadier General DUNCAN. 165th Brigade. Extract from LONDON GAZETTE. 2nd ROBERTS to be temp Lieut 23.9.15.	10 R. 10 R. 10 R. 10 R.

2449 Wt. W14957/M90 750,000 1/16 J.B.C. & A. Forms/C.2118/12.

WAR DIARY or INTELLIGENCE SUMMARY

Army Form C. 2118.

APRIL 1916 (2)   1/9th Batt. THE KINGS (Liverpool Regt.) T.F.

Instructions regarding War Diaries and Intelligence Summaries are contained in F.S. Regs, Part II and the Staff Manual respectively. Title Pages will be prepared in manuscript.

(Erase heading not required.)

Place	Date	Hour	Summary of Events and Information	Remarks and references to Appendices
BEAUMETZ LES LOGES.	13th		Weather fine. 2/Lt RUSSELL LATHAM evacuated to Hospital. Leave suspended today.	W.R.
		10.50pm	The Battalion relieved 1/5th KINGS on left front of F Sector. R.2. C.3.1. to M.19.b.9.2.5. the dispositions being C Coy on right, A Coy Centre, B Coy on left & D Coy in Support. The 1/5th KINGS on our right & the 1/6th Division on our left.	W.R.
	14th		Our other ranks wounded during relief. Weather wet. L/Cpl BRADBELT killed by sniper.	W.R. W.R. W.R.
			Works. Constructing Traverses, Coy Observation Post, & Trapboards Sentry Posts. wiring. Enemy quiet throughout the day. Weather wet.	W.R. W.R. W.R.
WAILLY.	15th			W.R.
	16th		Enemy Shelling front line & Support line during morning. Weather showery. Our Snipers had good results during the morning.	W.R. W.R.
	17th		Weather wet. 2/Lt W.H. CHALLINER & L/Cpl HALLIWELL evacuated to Hospital. Lt Col. C.G. BRADLEY DSO rejoined the Battalion from 3rd Army Conference.	W.R. W.R.
	18th	10.30pm	Our Lewis Guns dispersed enemy working party & pigeons at 3.45 AM. Weather wet.	W.R.
			3 Other ranks joined Battalion as reinforcements.	W.R.
	19th	2-30pm	The Battalion was relieved by 1/5th KINGS and moved into support at WAILLY. The strength from PETIT MODLIN and PETIT CHATEAU during garrison of our D Coy. Weather wet.	W.R.
	20th		5 Officers + 225 other Ranks on R.E. Fatigues. Daily.	W.R.
	21st		2/Lt RILEY + 10 other ranks proceeded to 165th Brigade Bombing Class at BEAUMETZ	W.R.
	22nd		Enemy machine guns active during night. Weather fine.	W.R.
	23rd		Weather fine. Enemy quiet.	W.R.
	24th		Weather fine. 2/Lt J.B. RUSSELL rejoined Battalion from Hospital. One other rank to Base wpt.	W.R.
			Weather showery. Enemy very quiet.	W.R.
	25th	2.30pm	The Battalion relieved the 1/5th KINGS on left front of F Sector R.24.C.2.1. to M19.b.9.2.5. the dispositions being A Coy on right, B Coy in Centre, D Coy on left & C Coy in Support. The 1/5 KINGS on our right and SOMERSET 1/4 Division on our left. The 1/5 KINGS took over trench 161 during their hour.	W.R.
			Lt FAWSSET proceeded to 165th Brigade HQrs for Humphrey duty. Weather fine.	W.R. W.R.
	26th		2 other ranks wounded. Weather fine. Our Snipers had good results during the day. Enemy shelled our front line & communication trenches.	W.R. W.R.
			Our other ranks killed and four wounded.	W.R.
	27th	2.30	Our Trench Mortar & Enemy Artillery very considerable damage. Weather fine. Enemy Artillery & M.G. active during night.	W.R. W.R.

2449 Wt. W14957/M90 750,000 1/16 J.B.C. & A. Forms/C.2118/12.

APRIL 1916   1/9th Battn THE KINGS. (Liverpool Regt) T.F.

Army Form C. 2118.

WAR DIARY
or
INTELLIGENCE SUMMARY
(Erase heading not required.)

Instructions regarding War Diaries and Intelligence Summaries are contained in F.S. Regs., Part II. and the Staff Manual respectively. Title Pages will be prepared in manuscript.

(3)

Place	Date	Hour	Summary of Events and Information	Remarks and references to Appendices
WAILLY	28th		Weather fine. Enemy exceptionally quiet.	WR.
	29th		Weather fine. Enemy quiet, excepting at night, and Machine Guns went fairly active. 2/Lt RICHERY 2/Lt HEENAN + two other ranks proceeded to Divisional School at GOUY.	WR. WR.
	30th		Enemy quiet during day. Weather fine. Lt.Col. Ct. BRADLEY DSO. proceeded to St Pol on Artillery Conference. Capt PGA. LEDERER assumed Command. One other rank wounded.	WR. WR. WR.

CBBradley Lt.Col
Commanding 1/9th Kings Regt
1/9th Kings Regt

WAR DIARY / INTELLIGENCE SUMMARY

Army Form C.2118

1/9th Batt. THE KING'S (Liverpool Regt) T.F.

MAY 1916

Place	Date	Hour	Summary of Events and Information	Remarks and references to Appendices
WAILLY	1st		Weather fine. Enemy quiet throughout the day.	10 R.
		11-30pm	The Battalion was relieved by 1/5 KINGS and marched to Billets at BEAUMETZ.	10 R.
Trenches BEAUMETZ	2nd		Weather changeable. Cleaning equipment, billets etc. The Battn found working parties as 1 Officer & 70 O.R. Burying Cable etc.	10 R.
	3rd		Weather fine.	10 R.
			Inoculation commenced for all men who had not been inoculated during last 18 months.	10 R.
	4th		Weather fine. Training carried out in Bathing, Musketry & Route March.	10 R.
	5th		Weather fine.	10 R.
			Col G. BRADLEY D.S.O. rejoined Battn from Artillery Conference and resumed command.	10 R.
	6th		Weather fine.	10 R.
	7th		Weather changeable. Church Parade.	10 R.
	8th		Weather changeable.	10 R.
		11-30pm	The Battn relieved the 1/5 KINGS in front line, left front of F Sector. R.34 c.2.1. and 19 to 95.50. Dispositions from Coys being B Coy on the right, D Coy in the centre, C Coy on the left & A Coy in support. Each Coy in front line had one platoon in support line. The b/5 SOMERSETS in Division were on our left & the 1/5 KINGS on our right.	10 R. (Fitzhenry M) 1-10pm 10 R.
WAILLY	9th		Enemy very quiet. 1 Other Rank accidentally wounded. Weather wet.	10 R.
	10th	8 am	Enemy very quiet during the morning. During the afternoon 2 chilled Communication Trenches and Support line. Enemy shelled Left Front Coy. Our trench mortars fired on Enemy working party at M.19.b.65.15. Weather fine.	10 R. 10 R.
	11th		1 Officer found Batt. as reinforcements (from Base) (Hospital) Lt HALLIWELL. Enemy killed. Wood just behind WAILLY very heavily during early morning.	10 R. 10 R.
	12th		Weather fine. Enemy very quiet.	10 R.
		12 midnight	The 1/4 Batt DUKE CORNWALL L.I. relieved 6/5 SOMERSETS on our left. 1 Officer joined Battn as reinforcements (from Base) (Hospital) 2/Lt CHALLINER Work carried on during this tour i.e. shining, constructing Shell Slits & ark Gas first trenches.	10 R. 10 R. 10 R. 10 R. 10 R. 10 R.

MAY 1916 (3) 1/7th Battⁿ. THE KING'S (Liverpool Regt) T.F.

Army Form C. 2118.

WAR DIARY
or
INTELLIGENCE SUMMARY
(Erase heading not required.)

Instructions regarding War Diaries and Intelligence Summaries are contained in F. S. Regs., Part II. and the Staff Manual respectively. Title Pages will be prepared in manuscript.

Place	Date	Hour	Summary of Events and Information	Remarks and references to Appendices
WAILLY	13th		Weather wet. Enemy artillery active during morning and bombardment trenches. Machine guns active during night	
	14th		Weather fine. Enemy Artillery active during morning machine guns active at night. Captⁿ Goldbaker proceeded on leave for 7 days to Blighty.	
	15th	3.15pm	The Bath was returned by the 1/7th KINGS & proceeded to WAILLY village	
	16th		Weather fine	
			Weather fine	
			Working parties found for R.E.s & Brigade Signal officer, 12 Officers & 300 other Ranks. Normandy wire employed strengthening HQ & reforming Trenches in village & deepening communication Trenches	
	17th		A quiet day. Enemy mounted machine gun fire on village during night	
	18th		Weather fine	
	19th		Enemy's machine village during the afternoon	
			Weather fine	
			Several rifled missiles during the day. Gas Alert turned.	
	20th		Weather fine	
		9.30pm	50 men arrived from 1/5 Kings to be attached to Battⁿ temporarily	
	21st	3.30pm	The Battⁿ relieved the 1/7th KINGS and took over trenches from R.2 w.c. 2.1 to w.19.b 9.5.5 a disposition of Coys being D Coy on the right C Coy on the right, B Coy in support, each Coy and Platoon having two Lewis mgs on platoon in support. Kew 2.6.6 Company to the Division were in support having KINGS on our right	
	22nd		Weather fine 95 other Rs were attached by the DUKE CORNWALL'S L.I. Work continued on T&Cs & wiring	
	23rd		Weather fine 10 other Rs 1 OR killed Enemy Artillery active	

Army Form C. 2118.

1/9th Batt THE KINGS.
(Liverpool Regt) T.F.

WAR DIARY
or
INTELLIGENCE SUMMARY
(Erase heading not required.)

MAY 1916. (3)

Instructions regarding War Diaries and Intelligence Summaries are contained in F.S. Regs., Part II. and the Staff Manual respectively. Title Pages will be prepared in manuscript.

Place	Date	Hour	Summary of Events and Information	Remarks and references to Appendices
WAILLY	24th		Weather fine. 2/Lt Rance (1st KINGS attached) wounded. Lt NEWTON rejoined Battn from Base Hospital. Col C.G. BRADLEY DSO proceeded to England for Investiture & leave. Capt P.G. FEDERER assumed Command.	10 K. 10/18 KK
	25th		Weather fine. Enemy shelled PETIT CHATEAU & WAILLY.	10/18 10/18
	26th		Weather fine. Enemy shelled Battn HQ during Afternoon. 2 Lewis Guns arrived.	10/18 10/18 10/18
	27th		Weather fine. 10th Bn W NIGER T3, other Ranks wounded. Enemy shelled Support Line.	10/18 10/18 10/18 10/18
	28th		Weather fine. The Battn was relieved on the evening of the 28/29 by the 1st Cay Bgd being relieved at 10.35 pm & marched to Billets at BEAUMETZ.	10/18
BEAUMETZ	29th		Weather fine. 200 Other Ranks supplied for working Parties in a Covering Cottle Line & Burying Cable etc.	10/18 10/18
	30th		Weather fine. Training carried on with.	10/18
	31st		Weather fine. 6 Officers joined Battn as reinforcements. 2/Lt OLIVER, J.R. 2/Lt SEMPLE, F.J. 2/Lt KYDD, H.M. 2/Lt WILDE, E. 2/Lt JONES, M. 2/Lt HODROHAN, A.C. 2/Lt SHEPHERD	10/18 10/18 10/18 10/18 10/18 10/18

P.G. Federer Capt
Commanding 9th Kings

Army Form C. 2118

WAR DIARY or **INTELLIGENCE SUMMARY**

1/9th Battⁿ THE KINGS (Liverpool Regt) T.F.

(Erase heading not required.)

JUNE 1916

Place	Date	Hour	Summary of Events and Information	Remarks and references to Appendices
BEAUMETZ	June 1st		Training carried out while at rest. Weather fine.	W.R.
do	" 2nd		MAJOR GENERAL H.S. TUDWINE C.B. inspected the Battalion on the Chateau grounds. Divisional Band attended. Football matches played in the afternoon. Weather fine.	W.R.
WAILLY SECTOR	" 3rd	12-30pm	The Battalion relieved the 7th KINGS in Left F Sector taking the night of the 3rd/4th dispositions of Coys being C in the night, B Coy in the Centre, B Coy on the Left, with D Coy in Support. A & B Somersets on our Left & the 6th Kings on the Right.	W.R.
	" 4th		Enemy quiet. Weather fine.	W.R.
	" 5th		Enemy quiet. Weather fine.	W.R.
	" 6th		Work carried on:- Shell Shelters, wiring, grass cutting, making Dugouts & constructing Bomb Posts. Weather fine. Enemy quiet. 1 O.R. wounded.	W.R.
	" 7th		Enemy quiet. Weather fine.	W.R.
	" 8th		Weather fine.	W.R.
	" 9th		Enemy shelled Dressing Station otherwise quiet.	W.R.
	" 10th		Enemy quiet. Weather fine.	W.R.
	" 11th		Lt Col C.G. BRADLEY DSO returned from leave & assumed command of the Battⁿ. Enemy quiet. Weather fine.	W.R.
	" 12th	3pm	Enemy shelled front line north 17mm shells & support line with about 15. 5.9s. Weather fine.	W.R.
WAILLY VILLAGE	" 13th		The Battalion was relieved by the 7th Kings & proceeded into billets in WAILLY VILLAGE. Weather fine. Working Parties found for R.E. of 3 N.C.O. & 110 O.R. They were employed running Support line & making new Fire steps.	W.R. W.R.
	" 14th		L.Cpl. Killed "D" Coy Killed 1 D.R Kings attached 9th Kings. Enemy very quiet. Weather wet. Working Parties found as for the 13th.	W.R. W.R. W.R.
	" 15th		Enemy quiet. Weather wet. Working parties as for 13th.	W.R. W.R.
	" 16th		Enemy quiet. Weather wet. 40 O.R. of the South Lancs attached for two nights to enable us to provide 1 Officer & 150 O.R. for special carrying Party.	W.R. W.R. W.R.
	" 17th		Enemy very quiet. Weather fine. Carrying Party suffered as in the 16th. 3 O.R. wounded as Reinforcements.	W.R. W.R.

WAR DIARY or INTELLIGENCE SUMMARY

Army Form C. 2118.

1/9th Batt THE KINGS (Liverpool Regt) T.F.

JUNE 1916 (2)

Place	Date	Hour	Summary of Events and Information	Remarks and references to Appendices
WAILLY VILLAGE	18th		Enemy quiet. Weather fine. Special Carrying Party supplied of G.O.R. & 320 O.R. Working & Ration Party to Battalions as Reinforcements.	W.R. W.R. W.R. W.R.
	19th	2 PM	The Battalion relieved the 2/5 LANCASHIRE FUSILIERS of the 166 Inf Bde in "E" Sector from T.R. 3 & 9 20.85 to A.19.e 25.60 our dispositions being A Coy in the centre, D Coy on the left with C Coy in Support. The 8th IRISH were on our right & the 5th Kings on our left.	Fighting 1/10,000 W.R. W.R. W.R.
	20th		Enemy quiet. Weather fine. The 2nd Lieut J. Scottish relieved W.O.F. & Ir. 15th on our right. Trenches in this sector on whole but fairly good. 1. O.R. wounded.	W.R. W.R.
	21st 22nd 22nd 23rd 24th		Weather fine. There was slight shelling & T.M. Bombs were fired on our Communication Trenches & however enemy was quiet. 2/Lt WATSON joined Battalion as Reinforcement. Enemy quiet. Weather fine. Enemy quiet. Weather fine. Weather fine. Our Artillery commenced wire Cutting at 9 A.M until 12 Noon & 2 P.M. to 6 P.M. The enemy retaliated with 77 M/M shells & 5.9.a, falling mainly on our Communication Trenches Support Line & Battn H.Q. Battn H.Q. moved to dugouts that was under course of Construction. During night the enemy was very quiet.	W.R. W.R. W.R. W.R. W.R. W.R.
	25th	9.30PM	2 Officers joined as Reinforcement. At 9.30 PM Trench Mortars & at 10 PM to 12 Noon Artillery continued wire Cutting, two good lanes being made. Through enemy wire. At 2 PM - 2.45 PM our Artillery concentrated on enemy's trenches & was with good effect. The enemy retaliated on support line & Communication Trenches, very little damage being done. Our Machine trench guns fired continually throughout the night.	W.R. W.R.
	26th		Weather fine. Weather hot. Our Artillery & Trench Mortars concentrated on enemy's Trenches from 11 A.M. - 11.30 A.M. with good results. The enemy's retaliation was very weak indeed. Very little damage being done to our trenches. Our Artillery & T.M. concentrated on enemy Trenches from 2 PM - 2.30 PM with good results. There was a little more retaliation during the afternoon than there was this morning.	W.R.

WAR DIARY / INTELLIGENCE SUMMARY

Army Form C. 2118.

1/9th Batt. The Kings Liverpool Regt. T.F.

JUNE 1916 — (3)

Place	Date	Hour	Summary of Events and Information	Remarks and references to Appendices
WAILLY TRENCHES	27th	8AM & 2PM	Our Artillery opened fire on the enemy's trenches, with good effect. No retaliation was noticed. The enemy TMs [trench mortars] were active. Practically no damage was done to our trenches. During the afternoon about 12 5.9s were fired by the enemy at BRETONCOURT — WAILLY RD. During the night our Artillery bombarded villages of BLAIRVILLE & FICHEUX. Rt about 10.10 PM the enemy put about 8 "77mm" shells on our front line.	A.R. 10 F.P.
	28th		Weather fine.	
			An ALERT PERIOD ordered at 12.45 PM. ZERO hour 5 PM. At 5.00 PM "Cassagnan" worked out 2 ft of our front line trench while 5.35 PM Our Artillery also opened fire on the enemy's trenches at 5 PM. At 5.35 PM a raiding party of the 1/4th LOYAL NORTH LANCS left our trenches & advanced to R34.B.56. 10 PM They were held up by Machine gun & rifle grenade fire & were forced to retire. At 5.30 PM a raiding party of 2/5th LANCASHIRE FUS left our trenches & entered the German trenches at R34.B.98.65. 8 [?] enemy men were knocked out from front line trench & a party knocked about 10 yards into a Communication Trench. This party killed another 4 or 5 of enemy & saw some put up dugouts coming across the open. They killed a number of these dead probably killed by the enemy and quite a number were also dead evidently killed by our Artillery bombardment. Considerably from our bombardment. The Trenches had suffered	
			A party of men from our Battalion went over the trenches represented by the 5/6 King and entered the enemy Sap. R.29.B.7. They were roughly handled by enemy and they found the Sap dead enclosed until 30 yards. They then withdrew along the Sap side at the Sap & returned no enemy when the SAp terminated. At this point at entering the entrance to a dugout was found which was about 3 steps down. A bomb failed to damage this. This failed and they advanced down the Sap they were met in the bay. 2/Lt DARLING's party got the two German men with his revolver. It was immediately replied. A Lewis Gun advanced. He was shot and killed. 2/Lt DARLING was shelled above the parapet about that time. He was carried but our trenches were unable to face him. A party then got out to help found that these shells when the sig had unfortunately been wounded. The party	
			then returned to our trenches. On the hill being called it was found 2/Lt HARLEY were missing. 2/Lt DARLING then called for a volunteer, N.C.O #627 Pte WINROW then came forward. They returned to the German lines found Mr Riley's body. Pte WINROW was bombed & he suffered in getting away. They carried our casualties. On the raiding party were eight, being 2/Lt HARLEY 1 OR killed & OR wounded.	A.R. 10 F.P.

WAR DIARY or INTELLIGENCE SUMMARY

Army Form C. 2118.

June 1916 (4)

1/9 Batt'n King's Liverpool Reg't T.F.

Place	Date	Hour	Summary of Events and Information	Remarks and references to Appendices
WAILLY TRENCHES	28th		The Bombardment continued until 8.30 P.M. The enemy's retaliation was not very strong, & put up a barrage along our front line but very little damage was done - we only had one other casualty, in addition to those sustained on the road. During the night the enemy was very active. Keeping up a good fire by m. guns & rifles on our front, otherwise he was very quiet. 1 O.R. wounded. (in addition to the casualties on the road)	W.R. / W.R. W.R.
	29th		Our Artillery opened fire on the enemy's trenches at 1.30 P.M. & continued until 1.55 P.M. The shooting was pretty accurate, and a good deal of damage was done to the parapet. One gun was pretty accurately thrown into the air. The enemy's retaliation was weak. Our front line was damaged slightly. The Support Line & Communication trenches were blown in several places. 77 m/m still mainly being used. During the night our Artillery bombarded the village of BLAIRVILLE & FICHEUX. A few rifle shots after as the enemy were every now & again through out the night. It certainly was fairly quiet during the night.	W.R.
	30th		Our Artillery continued to do cutting between 8 A.M. & 12 NOON & between 2 P.M. & 4 P.M. Our limbers were 4.5 P.M. & 7 P.M. The shooting was pretty accurate & other two were made on the enemy's wire. The enemy retaliated about 1 P.M. north of our rebellers on the remainder of the day the enemy was fairly quiet.	W.R.

[signature]
Commanding 1/9 King's

165th Brigade.

55th Division.

1/9th BATTALION

THE KING'S LIVERPOOL REGIMENT

JULY 1916

Vol 15

War Diary
of the
1/9th Liverpool Regt.,
165th Infantry Brigade
55th (West Lancashire) Division
for the period
1st July, 1916 to 31st July, 1916.

Army Form C. 2118.

1/9th Batt. The Kings
(Liverpool Regt) T.F.

WAR DIARY
or
INTELLIGENCE SUMMARY
(Erase heading not required.)

- JULY -
1916

Instructions regarding War Diaries and Intelligence Summaries are contained in F. S. Regs., Part II. and the Staff Manual respectively. Title Pages will be prepared in manuscript.

Place	Date	Hour	Summary of Events and Information	Remarks and references to Appendices
WAILLY TRENCHES	1st		Weather fine. At 4.20pm our Artillery bombarded the enemy's trenches & continued doing considerable damage to his parapet. At 4.25pm we put up a smoke barrage. The enemy retaliated chiefly on our front line, smashing in the parapet in about 10 places. The support line & communication trenches were practically undamaged. 77m m shells were being used. At 11 AM we fired about 10. 6" shells at the enemy's trenches & replied with a few 77 m m shells. Remainder of day very quiet.	10 R
	2nd		Weather fine. During the morning the enemy shelled our front & support line & afterwards the parapet with 5.9s. At 1 PM they commenced to bombard our front & support line between A15 & Charli St. with 5.9s and 4.2s, doing considerable damage to our front & support, & continued until 3.35 PM. At 3.10 PM they commenced a rapid rate of fire on the same portion of our trenches which lasted until 4.10 PM after an interval of 20 minutes. The fire commenced again and continued until 5.30 PM. Three dugouts were blown in, two being a minor dug out shown on at head dugouts until 4.15 AM the following morning when all the men had been rescued, 9 of them being wounded. Both were covered. Our retaliation on the enemy's trenches appeared to be rather weak, but the enemy did very good work, & was reported Ry had damaged the village of FICHEUX except for our G companies of Ry 1st DEVONS moved into our reserve line ready to assist if necessary. At about 9.30 PM 2 K Coy & 1 Coy of KINGS attached to DEVONS. During the night every effort was made to repair damage done to our front line. Two Platoons of Ry 1st SOUTH LANCS the 9th KINGS & the two Platoons of the 1st SOUTH LANCS assisting.	10 R 10 R 10 R 10000 FICHEUX 10 R 10 R 10 R 10 R
		5 PM 9.30 PM	Casualties 2/Lt E Jones & 6 OR killed. 10 OR wounded. 3 subsequently died from wounds. Casualties of 1st KINGS attached to the Battn. 2 OR killed + 30 R wounded. 1 major & C. Coy, attached D. Coy. in the front line. (Right Coy) The enemy were fairly quiet throughout the night.	10 R 10 R 10 R 10 R

WAR DIARY or INTELLIGENCE SUMMARY

— JULY 1916 —   19 Batn. The Kings (Liverpool Regt.) T.F.

Place	Date	Hour	Summary of Events and Information	Remarks and references to Appendices
WAILLY TRENCHES	3rd		Weather fine. B.O.R. wounded.	WR WR
		3.58PM	The enemy was very quiet during the day until 3.58PM when he put about 30 77mm shells onto our Support line. During the night he fired occasional salvoes on our working parties. The C.O. & 4th Kings returned to Bretencourt at 10 AM. The two platoons of the 14th South Lancs remained in our Trenches.	WR WR WR
	4th		A working party of 160 O.R. furnished supplies to assist us in during the trenches. Weather changeable. Except for a few 77mm shells the enemy was very quiet throughout the day. During the night he fired occasional salvoes on our working parties.	WR WR WR
		1.30PM	The two platoons of the 14th South Lancs went out to Trench. A working party of 120 O.R. furnished supplies to assist us in during the Trenches. 160 O.R. joined the Battn as reinforcements. 48 & 1/0 6th Kings & 55 of the 1st Kings.	WR WR WR WR WR
	5th		Weather fine. The enemy fired occasional shells on our front & Support lines during the day. Observers very quiet. 100 O.R. Pioneers were working on our trenches during the night.	WR WR WR WR
	6th		Weather fine. Enemy quiet.	WR WR
			139 O.R. joined Battn as reinforcements. 1 Offr & 54 Kings, 7 7th Kings, 43 5th Kings 59 9th Kings & 17/10th Kings.	WR WR
	7th		Weather fine. Enemy quiet.	WR WR
		9PM	GAS ALERT ordered.	WR
		4PM	GAS ALERT cancelled. A party of 60 O.R. were working in our Trenches during night.	WR WR
	8th		Weather fine. Enemy quiet.	WR WR

Army Form C. 2118.

19th Batt. The King's
Liverpool Regt. T.F.

WAR DIARY
or
INTELLIGENCE SUMMARY

(Erase heading not required.)

JULY 1916 — (3)

Instructions regarding War Diaries and Intelligence Summaries are contained in F. S. Regs., Part II. and the Staff Manual respectively. Title Pages will be prepared in manuscript.

Place	Date	Hour	Summary of Events and Information	Remarks and references to Appendices
WAILLY TRENCHES	8th	2.20 P.M.	The Battn was relieved by the 6th King's and marched to BEAUMETZ. Tea was served in the CHATEAU grounds. At 9 P.M. they proceeded to entrain at GOUY arriving there at 10.15 P.M.	10 R
S. GOUY	9th		Weather fine. 55. O.R. Rifles were inspected by the Armourer Sergt. Church parade was held at 11.15 A.M. in the Camp grounds.	10 R
	10th		Weather fine. The Battn carried out practice in the attack, during the morning and afternoon, at Dummy trenches. Officers to mark the Battn as reinforcements. 2Lt P.A.GUMMER. 2Lt R.M.POOLEY. 2Lt Lt. G.PRITCHARD. 2Lts. NELSON-SMITH, HOTBYRNE, 2nd CUR HILL. 2Lt R.E. WILDE. 2/Lt W.L.S.RATH.	10 R
	11th		Weather fine. During the morning practice in the attack was continued. In the afternoon the Battn went on a route march.	10 R
	12th		Weather Changeable. The same programme as for the 10th.	10 R
	13th		Weather Changeable. Programme as for the 10th.	10 R
	14th		Weather Changeable. Programme of training as for the 10th.	10 R
	15th		Brakes and 55. S.R. (Scottish) gave an entertainment. Strict guard orders & practice alarm of having a guard.	10 R
	16th		Weather fine. 60. O.R joined as reinforcements. Church Parade.	10 R
	17th		Wet weather.	10 R
	18th		Battn inspection by Brig. Gen. Duncan C.M.G. in the attack.	10 R
	19th		Programme of training as for the 10th. Weather fine.	10 R

WAR DIARY or INTELLIGENCE SUMMARY

July 1916   1/9 Bath Sayforth (Liverpool Regt) JF.

Army Form C.2118.

(Erase heading not required.)

Instructions regarding War Diaries and Intelligence Summaries are contained in F.S. Regs., Part II. and the Staff Manual respectively. Title Pages will be prepared in manuscript.

Place	Date	Hour	Summary of Events and Information	Remarks and references to Appendices
GOUY	19th		Weather fine. Training carried out as for Ro. 10th	WR AR 10R
SUS-ST LEGER	20th	7AM	The Batt. proceeded to billets at SUS-ST LEGER, arriving at 10.45 A.M.	WR 10R
HAILLY	21st	7PM	Weather fine. Bath on reinforcements 70. 10th Kings. The Batt. proceeded to billets at HAILLY, arriving at 11 A.M.	WR 10R 4/15 R
AUTHEUX	22nd	7AM	Weather fine. Bath on reinforcements 43 - 5th Kings. 1 - 6th Kings. 1 - 2 Kings. also 2/4 PdM ORE ELAM & VICARY	WR 10R 12R
			So the Batt proceeded to AUTHEUX arriving at 12 NOON	
do	23rd		Weather fine. Church parade.	10R
do	24th		Weather fine. Training carried out in morning & Route March during the afternoon.	10R 10R
do	25th		Weather fine. Training carried out in morning & Route March during the afternoon. The Battn was inspected by the Brigadier Gen. Duncan DSO.	10R 10R
			The following M.O.'s men were decorated by the Brigadier Gen Duncan DSO.	
			R.S.M. MILLER, MILITARY CROSS. No. 3023 Sgt HALL. No. 3410 CoPl WARNER. No. 3181 CoPl HYLAND. No. 3630 PtR N 9 PIER R.R. MILITARY MEDAL. Rifles being given to each.	10R
		5PM	The Battn proceeded to CANDAS to entrain. Owing to the train being late we did not entrain until 1.30 A.M.	
MERICOURT	26th		The Battn arrived at MERICOURT at 6 A.M. After detraining they marched to billets in the village.	10R WR
do	27th		Weather fine.	10R 62D 10R 6R
do	28th	3.5PM	Weather fine. Training carried out. The Battn proceeded to BUSNES area at K. 17B + K 11D arriving at 6 P.M.	WR 6R
K 17 B + K 11 D	29th		Weather fine. Training carried out.	WR 6R

WAR DIARY
or
INTELLIGENCE SUMMARY

1/9 Batt THE KINGS (Liverpool Regt) T.F.

July 1916

Place	Date	Hour	Summary of Events and Information	Remarks and references to Appendices
K17 B + K17 D	30.	3.45 PM	Weather fine. The Batt proceeded to Bivouac area at F14D.	
F14 D + F20A	31st		Weather fine. Coy Training carried out.	

C Shuttle
Lt Col
Commanding 1/9 Kings

165th Brigade.
55th Division.

1/9th BATTALION

THE KING'S LIVERPOOL REGIMENT

AUGUST 1916

WAR DIARY or INTELLIGENCE SUMMARY

Army Form C. 2118.

1/9th Battn THE KING'S (L'pool Regt) T.F.

Month: AUGUST Year: 1916

Place	Date	Hour	Summary of Events and Information	Remarks and references to Appendices
Bivouac Area F20 B. F23 A	1st.	9 AM	The Battalion proceeded to new Bivouac Area at F23A	10R * to R6.3D NE.
	2nd		Weather fine. Practice at the Attack carried out.	10R 10R
	3rd		Weather fine. Training carried out.	10R 10R
	4th		Weather fine.	10R
TRONES WOOD SECTOR	4th	4.30 PM	Battn. moved from Bivouac area at F23a and relieved the 8th Battn THE KING'S OWN in Support to 2/5 Lancashire Fusiliers at the BRIQUETERIE. Dispositions of Companies being "B" Coy were in close support in trench from A6a 1 & b 5.30 & 00.05, just South of TRONES WOOD. The remaining three companies were in trench South of BERNAFAY WOOD. Battalion Headquarters were established at the BRIQUETERIE.	GUILLEMONT 57100 10R
	5th	3 AM	Relieved 2/5 LANCASHIRE FUSILIERS in the front line dispositions of our Companies being A Coy on left just South of TRONES WOOD. B Coy on the right. D Coy in Support. C Coy in Battalion Headquarters being at S 30 a 5.3. Shelled commenced at 3 PM & continued S.30.00 us Battalion Headquarters & the Brickfields marked B.M. During the rest of evening shelled to enemy observation & was accomplished much damage and inflicting numerous communication trenches. The Support trenches this time & continued casualties. Battalion Headquarters were heavily shelled. During 4/5 "B" Company caused 177 M.M. & 5.9 but many S.Q. shells thrown were decided to shore trench to the sunken road which has been continuously bombarded. If was moved by C.O. and immediately began manning along the side of the road. The trench was of mounds of casualties.	GUILLEMONT 57100 10R
	5/6			10R 10R
	6th		Weather fine Enemy continued to shell our position throughout the day. At 10 AM or nearly 18 sick were again evacuated. Dispositions were now: "B" being brought into our "B" Battalion Headquarters again about 8.30 C Coy & D Coy to relieve Battalion & "B" Coy & Coy in evening, all the two forward companies to each relieved some time in the sunken road near Captain WORDERSON & 2 others were wounded. Relieving Battalion was 6 LC COCKRAN. 9/10 WILDERN. 2/Lt PRITCHARDLEY & 93 O.R. Jumbo as casualties.	GUILLEMONT 57100 10R
	7/16		During the day and during the night 7/8 Aug a new command of trench from SUNKEN ROAD through to TRONES WOOD—GUILLEMONT ROAD. Commenced under the first line.	GUILLEMONT 57100 10R

WAR DIARY or INTELLIGENCE SUMMARY

Army Form C. 2118.

1/9th Battalion THE KINGS (Liverpool Regt.) T.F.

AUGUST 1916

Place	Date	Hour	Summary of Events and Information	Remarks and references to Appendices
TRONES WOOD SECTOR	7th	11.30 (P.M)	The Battalion was relieved by the 8th IRISH, 4th KINGS OWN and 4th NORTH LANCS and proceeded to the NE corner of OXFORD COPSE and hence to old British heavy gun road of the TALUS BOISÉ at A.9.c.9.6.	GUILLEMONT 1:20,000 10 R.
TALUS BOISÉ A.9.c.9.6	8th		Weather fine. Baths in Reserve in old British line, making wire entanglements.	10 F. 10 R.
	9th		Weather fine. Battalion in Reserve in old British line, making wire entanglements.	10 F. 10 R.
			Weather fine. 8th HENSHIL WOOD. A.R. 8/8 AM B.D.AMS. Surrounded the Baths as reinforcements.	
	10th	9-30 PM	A Coy proceeded to EDWARDS TRENCH. Remainder took over COCHRANE ALLEY. "B" Coy. proceeded to CASEMENT TRENCH at 9-30 p.m. we were to 10th KINGS. The above Companies came under orders of OC 6th KINGS.	GUILLEMONT 1:20,000 10 R.
	11th		During the night of 11/12th the Battalion took over trenches from 6th KINGS from COCHRANE ALLEY on the right to the junction of SHUTE TRENCH with ASSEMBLY TRENCH on the left. The dispositions of Coys were "C" & "D" Coys in the front line, "A" & "D" Coys in the ASSEMBLY TRENCH, Battalion Headquarters being "A" & "D" Coys in the road and "C" & "D" Coys in COCHRANE ALLEY, Battalion Headquarters D at the Lt. Battalion Bombers filling the Block in COCHRANE ALLEY. Battalion snipers established at junction of MALTZ HORN Trench and DUNCAN ALLEY.	GUILLEMONT 1:20,000 10 R.
			Weather fine.	
MALTZ HORN FARM AREA	13th		The enemy shelled our trenches during the morning. In the course of the afternoon orders were received that the Battalion would attack at 5.15 P.M. in conjunction with the Brigade along a line running from E.1.C.3035 northwards with 41st Div. then operating back on our right. Our Objective was to advance 150 to 200 yards and then settle down at that line. "A" Bn joined up with our original front line. One Coy "B" was detailed to support "A" Bn in the advance 1/2 of Coy to the left and 1/4 section of the Battalion Bombers went to advance into COCHRANE ALLEY and take a Block. "C" & "D" Coys were to support in ASSEMBLY TRENCH H. Own bombardment commenced at 3.30 P.M. and was vigorously replied to by the enemy. At 5.15 P.M - until about 7 P.M. our own continuous bombardment. At 5.15 P.M. "C" & "D" Coys then moved up into SHUTE TRENCH & after "A" Coy had moved into our front line. "C" & "D" Coys then attacked in two waves, our "C" & "D" Coys then commenced to concentrate their difficulty and was further assisted by B Coy who had moved up from the right. The hostile fire was commanded by a heavy barrage of NCOs and Pay Coy Coys & Coys and B Coy & position commenced to consolidate their difficulty was further completed at about 6.15 P.M. and at about 6.30 P.M. our position was enveloped by hundreds of C Coy. Jun Hawkins & Fred were wounded as was Lt Hutton along with another Subaltern.	GUILLEMONT 1:20,000 AR

Army Form C. 2118.

WAR DIARY or INTELLIGENCE SUMMARY

(Erase heading not required.)

- AUGUST 1916 -
1/10 Battalion THE KINGS (Liverpool Regt.) T.F.

Place	Date	Hour	Summary of Events and Information	Remarks and references to Appendices
MALTZ HORN FARM AREA	14th		The Battalion Bombers advanced to COCHRANE ALLEY and their objective was quickly reached by bombing others was killed immediately by machine gun fire. Two Scouts near the head were completely blown up and it was decided to withdraw down COCHRANE ALLEY and form a block. At 6-30 p.m. owing to casualties all available stretcher bearers were ordered to Advance Trenches and 400 stretchers of "C" Coy moved into COCHRANE ALLEY and formed an Advanced Flank. At 11.45 p.m. our advanced bomb had to withdraw to the old front line owing to the enemy outflanking our bombers and there being no one to either flank. The block in COCHRANE ALLEY continued to be held. During the severe bombardment telephone communication was maintained until 6.50 p.m. After this hour the whole system of Wires were frequently destroyed and communication was kept up by means of runners.	GUILLEMONT 20,000
	15th	6.30 p.m.	Weather fine. The Battn was relieved by 1/10 Battalion THE KINGS (L'pool Regt) T.F. and proceeded to Bivouac area F22.A arriving at 10 p.m.	
F22.A VILLE-SUR-ANCRE	14th	3 p.m.	Sent to following additional casualties from 9th inst. Read army Form B [illegible] Capt WM FULTON. 2/Lt WATSON. 3/Lt WOOD. POWELL. NO. 1368 GUNNER 2Lt STEWART LOUGH ... &c. Capt R POOLEY. SHEPPARD WHITEHEAD R. &c. 3/GtJTR SEMPLE SHEPPARD. 3/LR MACKENZIE [illegible] OR MARRIOTT. 3/LR TOWER MITCHELL HULSE. The Battln proceeded to Billets at VILLE-SUR-ANCRE.	
	15th	6.30 p.m.	Weather fine. Battln were inspected by the Mayor General Commanding Division.	
	16th		Weather fine. Training etc.	
	17th		Weather fine. Training etc.	
	18th	4 p.m.	The Commandant &c. proceeded to new billeting area to catch train. The RC Chaplain joined Battln as reinforcement.	

WAR DIARY or INTELLIGENCE SUMMARY

Army Form C. 2118.

19th Battalion THE KING'S or (L'pool Regt) T.F.

AUGUST 1916

Place	Date	Hour	Summary of Events and Information	Remarks and references to Appendices
VILLE-SUR-ANCRE.	19th	8.45 p.m.	Weather fine. The Battalion proceeded to MERICOURT Station and entrained for MARTAINVILLE, arriving there at 6 p.m. and marched to RAMBURELLES.	M.R. at BEVILLE 111 DIEPPE. 16
RAMBURELLES	20th		Weather fine.	Dispersed R.P.
	21st		Weather fine. Coy and Battalion training carried out while at RAMBURELLES.	10 R.
	22nd		Weather fine.	10 R.
	23rd		Weather fine. 2/Lt G. NELSON-SMITH admitted to Hospital (sick)	10 R.
	24th		Weather fine.	10 R.
			2/Lt A.C. SHEPHERD rejoined the Battalion from the 165 Trench Mortar Battery.	10 R.
	25th		Weather fine.	10 R.
			2/Lt T.E.S. JONES admitted to Hospital (sick)	10 R.
			2/Lt H.W. NEWTON posted to 165 Trench Mortar Battery.	10 R.
	26th		Weather fine. The following joined the Battalion as reinforcements. 48 O.R. 4th Kings. 51 O.R. 9th Kings. 4.2 7th Kings, 35 8th Kings, 109 10th Kings.	10 R.
	27th		Battalion training & needs returned to their Unit.	10 R.
	28th		Lt Col C.G. BRADLEY. D.S.O. admitted to Hospital (sick). Major P.G. LEDERLE M.C. assumed command of the Battn.	10 R.
	29th		2/Lt L.L.S. RICHER, 2/Lt W.G. PRITCHARD admitted to Hospital (sick)	10 R.
	30th	10 a.m.	The Battalion proceeded to PONT-REMY and entrained for MERICOURT arriving there at 5 p.m. at E14D.	10 R.
	31st	7.30 a.m.	The Battalion marched from MERICOURT Station to Bivouac area at E14D arriving at 7.30 a.m.	10 R.
		3 p.m.	The Battalion proceeded to & took over billets at DERNANCOURT. Weather fine.	M.R.

[signature]

Major
Commanding 19th Battalion
THE KING'S (L'pool Regt) T.F.

9th King's (Liverpool Regiment)-

To   165th Infantry Brigade.

August 4th.   Battalion moved from bivouac area at F.23.a, and
        and relieved the 8th Battn "The King's" (Liverpool Regt),
        who were in support to 2/5th Lancs. Fusiliers at the
        BRIQUETERIE.   "B" Company were in close support in trench
        from A.6.a.1.6. to S.30.c.0.40, just South of TRONES WOOD.
        The remaining three Companies were in trench South of
        BERNFAY WOOD. Battalion bombers were along SUNKEN ROAD,
        S.E. of BRIQUETERIE. Battalion headquarters were
        established at the BRIQUETERIE.

August 5th.   The Battalion relieved 2/5th Lancs. Fusiliers in
        the front line, Battalion Headquarters being at S.30.a.5.3.
        The relief commenced at 2 p.m., but owing to enemy observation
        it was not completed until 8 p.m.   The enemy bombarded our
        Trenches vigourously with 77 mm, 4.2, but mainly 5.2 shells
        doing considerable damage and inflicting numerous casualties.
        Battalion headquarters were heavily shelled. Owing to "D"
        Coy being in the open on the SUNKEN ROAD, which was being
        continuously shelled, it was decided to dig a trench along the
        side of the road. This trench was completed by "D" Coy, and
        undoubtedly saved many casualties.

August 6th.   Enemy continued to bombard our position throughout
        the day.   At 10 am. a number of 8" shells were dropped near
        Battalion Headquarters, Headquarter being blown in. Headquarter
        were moved to a cubby hole on the Sunken Road at about S.30.c.
        5/5.
            Up to date the Battalion had sustained the following losses
        since taking over the front line.-
            4 officers 120 other ranks .
        During the day, and under heavy shell fire ' D ' Company dug
        a new Communication Trench from SUNKEN ROAD through the TRONES
        WOOD - GUILLEMONT Road " G.H " Trench joining up the front
        line. The Battalion was relieved at 11-30 pm. by the 8th.
        Irish, 4th. King's Own and 4th. N. Lancs. and proceeded to N.E.
        Corner of OXFORD COPSE and thence to old British Line just
        E. of TALUS BOISE, at A.9.c.9/6.

August 8th.   Battalion in Reserve in old British Line making wire
        entanglements.

August 9th.   Battalion in Reserve making wire entanglements etc.

August 10th.   'A' Company proceeded to EDWARDS TRENCH, Bombers
        took over COCHRANE ALLEY.   ' B ' Company proceeded to CASEMENT
        TRENCH at 9-30 pm. in Reserve to 6th. King's. The above
        Companies came under the orders of the O. C. 6th. King's.

August 11th.   During night 11/12th. Battalion took over trenches
        from 6th. King's from COCHRANE ALLEY on the right to Junction
        of SHUTE TRENCH, with Assembly Trench on the left.   The
        disposition being A & B. Companies in the Front Line, C & D
        Companies in the Assembly Trench - 'C' on the right ' D '
        on the left.   Battalion bombers holding the block in
        COCHRANE ALLEY. Battalion headquarters were established at
        junction of MALTZ HORN TRENCH with DUNCAN ALLEY.

August 12th.   The enemy shelled our position during the morning.
        In the course of the afternoon orders were received that the
        Battalion would attack at 5-15 p.m. in conjunction with the
        French, along a line running from B.1.c.20.85, northwards
        with its left flank bending back in a North Westerly direction

so that it could be joined up with our original front line.
One Company was detailed to join this up at night. "A" and
"B" Coy's were detailed to attack, "A" on the right and
"B" on the left.   Three sections of the Battalion bombers
were to advance up COCHRANE ALLEY and create a block.
"C" and "D" Coy's were in support in assembly trench.
Our bombardment commenced at 3-30 p.m. and was vigourously
replied to by the enemy.   From 5-15 p.m. until about
7 p.m. our artillery fire was intense. "A" and "B"
Coy's attacked in two waves, our "C" and "D" Companies then
moved up into SHUTE TRENCH.   Although "A" Coy lost their
Company Commander and 3 Platoon commanders, and "B" Coy,
3 Platoon commanders together with a heavy percentage of
N.C.Os, they reached their objective at about 5-45 p.m.
and commenced to consolidate.   Great difficulty was
experienced owing to hostile machine gun fire and rifle fire,
which was kept up all night.   At 6 p.m. one platoon
of "C" Coy was ordered to reinforce "A" coy, at 6-20 p.m. one
platoon of "D" Coy was ordered to reinforce "B" Coy.
Two platoons of FRED were then ordered up into SHUTE TRENCH
followed shortly afterwards by another two platoons.
The Battalion bombers advanced up COCHRANE ALLEY and their
objective was quickly reached, The Bombing Officer was killed
immediately on reaching the road.   This trench near the road
was completely blown in and it was decided to withdraw some
35 to 40 yards down COCHRANE ALLEY and form a block.   At
6-30 p.m. owing to casualties all available bombers were
ordered to reinforce the Battalion bombers and 2 Platoons of
"C" Coy moved into COCHRANE ALLEY and formed a defensive flank.
At 11-45 p.m. our advanced line had to withdraw to the old
front line owing to the enemy enfilading our position and there
being no one on either flank.   The block in COCHRANE ALLEY
continued to be held.   Despite the severe bombardment,
telephonic communication was maintained until 6-50 p.m.
At this hour the whole system of wires was practically
destroyed and communication was kept up by means of runners.

August 13th.   The Battalion was relieved by the 10th Battn "The
King's" (Liverpool Regt) at 6-30 p.m. and proceeded to
bivouac area F.23.a, arriving at 10 p.m.   Since 6/8/16 the
following additional casualties had been sustained :-
    11 Officers, 159 Other Ranks,
making a total of 15 Officers, 289 Other Ranks for the period
5th to 13th August 1916.

                                (sd) C. G. BRADLEY, Lieut-Colonel,
21/8/16.   9th "King's" Liverpool Regt.

KL 17

War Diary.

of

1/9th King's Liverpool Regt.

1st September to 30th September 1916

Army Form C. 2118.

WAR DIARY
or
INTELLIGENCE SUMMARY

(Erase heading not required.)

1/9th Batt'n THE KINGS (L'pool Regt) TF

SEPTEMBER 1916

Instructions regarding War Diaries and Intelligence Summaries are contained in F. S. Regs., Part II and the Staff Manual respectively. Title Pages will be prepared in manuscript.

Place	Date	Hour	Summary of Events and Information	Remarks and references to Appendices
DERNANCOURT	1st		Weather fine. Whilst in this village the Batt'n practised digging Strong Points etc.	W.R.
	2nd		Weather fine.	W.R.
	3rd		Weather Changeable.	W.R.
	4th		2/Lt Ho DANIEL & 2/Lt CR. HILL admitted to hospital. The Batt'n proceeded to the trenches taking over HKS WOODHOUSE'S KING'S 1200 on command of the Battalion.	W.R. W.R. W.R.
MONTAUBAN ALLEY Reserve Trenches		2.30 P.M.	They arrived at FIDA for dinner. We arrived at MONTAUBAN ALLEY at 5 P.M. and remained there in reserve. Disposition of our Companies being B Coy on the right, A Coy in the Centre Coy, D Coy left Centre Coy, C Coy on the left. Batt'n Bombers in the Redoubt Overland at S.9 c 1.2. & Batt'n H.Qrs at S.9 d 7.10.15. The enemy shelled Batt'n HQ with about 12 tr's shortly after we arrived.	W.R.
	5th		Weather wet. 2/Lt THE MONSEIGH reported the Battalion from hospital & took Carswell but making himself deficient. Casualties: 1. O.R. KILLED.	W.R. W.R. W.R.
	6th		Weather wet. 1. O.R. Wounded.	W.R.
	7th	6 Am	Weather Changeable. The Batt'n proceeded to the front line & relieved the 7 KINGS. Disposition of our Coys being "D" Coy on the right. "C" Coy in the Centre, B Coy on the left & A Coy in support in ORCHARD Trench. The Batt'n HQrs in CARLTON TRENCH. Bombers were in SAVOY Trench & Batt'n HQrs at SH 85.6. "D" Coy also took over two Strong Points at S12 A 6 5 was at S12 A 5.3 and the left at SH 85.6. "D" Coy took over on Strong Point at S12.9.7 During the & S12 A 6 respectively. "C" Coy took over on Strong Point at S12.9.7. During the day the enemy was fairly quiet. At night work was commenced connecting up the Strong Points, digging a communication trench along the FLERS R'd from the front line to the Right Strong Point, also extending our left to try and get in touch with the 5 KINGS. Why. Trench was dug for 130 yards 3 ft deep. Our left then rested on NORTH ST. at a point about S 8 c 7.0 Three wire patrols by one of our patrols during the night	W.R.

Army Form C. 2118.

WAR DIARY or INTELLIGENCE SUMMARY

1/9 Batt'n THE KINGS (L'pool Regt) T.F.

(Erase heading not required.)

Place	Date	Hour	Summary of Events and Information	Remarks and references to Appendices
TEA TRENCH	7th Sept. Cont'd		A patrol was sent up the FLERS Rd for a distance of 350 yds and found it was not occupied by the enemy. A patrol went out in the direction of S11.a.9.8. but could find no sign of the enemy. A patrol also went out and got in touch with the 5th KINGS & reported TEA TRENCH was not occupied by the enemy. A Coy athwartside moved up into the left centre. "B" Coy moving along into position. 2. O.R. Killed. Brigade was on our right. The 5th KINGS on our left.	LONGUEVAL 1/20,000 10 R.e.
			The 166th Inf. Brigade was on our right. The 5th KINGS on our left. Casualties. 2. O.R. Killed. 3. O.R. wounded. v 1. O.R. missing. Weather fine.	10 R.e. 10 R.e.
	8th		During the day the enemy kept up an intense arty. barrage (which at times was very intense) along a line DELVILLE WOOD. ORCHARD TRENCH, PEAR TRENCH, WOOD LANE. At night our "D" Coy took over a strong point at S11B.95 from the 10th SCOTTISH. took over carried on consolidating up all the line. Strong points in also bombarded the trench from NORTH St. 80yds in a WESTERLY direction. APPLE TRENCH was also defended. A patrol went up the FLERS Rd for about 300yds from junction of Roads S12 a 55.36 along Road towards FLERS & found none of the enemy. A patrol of 1 Officer & 4 O.R. Bombers left our trench about S11B55 & proceeded in a NW direction & when about 100yds NW of this point the enemy opened fire with two MG's from a point about S11B.9.8. Killing the Cpl.. The patrol returned shortly afterwards and reported this. A patrol went along TEA TRENCH in a westerly direction & found trenches in it. The 5th KINGS. They reported the trench much knocked about & dead bodies in it. At intervals during the night the enemy put up two heavy barrages. Casualties. 1. O.R. Killed. 13. O.R. wounded.	LONGUEVAL 1/20,000 10 R.e. 10 R.e. 10 R.e.
	9th		Our "C" & "D" Coys were relieved in the front line by two Coys of the 4th KINGS. They also took over the strong points. Our relief "C" & "D" Coys proceeded to CARLTON TRENCH where they remained in reserve. Two platoons of A Coy were withdrawn from the front line & put into ORCHARD trench. At intervals through out the day and night the enemy put up two heavy barrages. At about 5.10 P.M. one of two MG's at S11B.40.A.S. opened an enemy MG in a shell hole about S.11B.25.80 on NORTH ST. which was firing in the direction of WOODLANE. Our shell fire on it and	10 R.e. LONGUEVAL 1/20,000 10 R.e. 10 R.e. LONGUEVAL 1/20,000 10 R.e.

2449 Wt. W14957/M90 750,000 1/16 J.B.C. & A. Forms/C.2118/12.

Army Form C. 2118.

1/9th Battn THE KINGS (L'pool Regt) T.F.

WAR DIARY
or
INTELLIGENCE SUMMARY

(Erase heading not required.)

SEPTEMBER 1916

Place	Date	Hour	Summary of Events and Information	Remarks and references to Appendices
TEA TRENCH	9th		Altogether 7 Lewis Guns which were firing from a parapet others our Stretcher cut NORTH ST. Silenced the enemy's M.G. Later on about 5-30 PM a number of Germans without arms (probably prisoners) broke away from the direction of WOODLANE and ran towards COFFEE TRENCH. Our Lewis M.Gs. were able to make good practice and reached the parties causing many casualties. Their parties got into shell holes and during the evening and night a number of rest flares were sent up. It is probable that owing to think length held against the enemy did not shell our front line being afraid of killing their own men. At the same time our inability to complete our work of connecting up the strong point with the trench line continuing the digging of the new trench & joining up with the old TEA Trench on our left at S 11 A. 4.5.	LONGUEVAL 1:20,000 2/19
			Casualties. 1 O.R. Killed 6 O.R. wounded	10/KR 10/K.R.
	10th		Weather fine. Throughout the day, at intervals the enemy put his own naval barrage. During the night of 10/11 "A" & "D" Coys were relieved in the front line by the 1st NEW ZEALAND Rifle Bde. The Battn Bombers & "D" Coys were relieved by the 3rd NEW ZEALAND Rifle Bde. in CARLTON SAVOY TRENCHES. The Corps marched independently back to Bivouac area at F 13 a.	10/KR 62DNE 10/KR 10/KR
F 13 a	11th	11AM	Casualties 1 O.R. KILLED. 5 O.R. wounded. During the day the Battn proceeded to BUIRE-SOUS-CORBIE & went under canvas.	10/KR 10/KR
BUIRE	12th		Weather fine.	10/KR 10/KR
	13th		Coy & Bn cleaning up. Drafts arriving from base where it had been training drafts for the last 2 months. Weather changeable. Coy training carried out.	10/KR

WAR DIARY or INTELLIGENCE SUMMARY

Army Form C. 2118.

19th Batt THE KING'S (Liverpool Regt.) T.F.

SEPTEMBER 1916

Place	Date	Hour	Summary of Events and Information	Remarks and references to Appendices
BUIRE	14th		Weather fine.	WR
	15th		Weather fine.	WR
	16th		Weather fine.	WR 6 DNE.
		2.30 P.M.	The Batt. proceeded to Buire area at E.15.A.	WR
			At about 6.30 P.M. the enemy shelled the Camp & the Battalion moved to another area in E.14.D.	WR
E.14.D	17th	11 A.M.	Weather fine	WR
			The Battalion proceeded to the trenches. Rallying at POMMIER REDOUBT for dinners, we remained there until 4.30 P.M. then continuing the march to the trenches. We relieved the 11th QUEENS in the front line the right being N31B 4.1 the left N31B 5.2. The disposition of our Coys being Batt. Bombers on the right. A Coy in the Centre. D Coy on the left.	MAP NO M.4 1/10,000
			B Coy being detailed to dig strong points in front of this line viz N.35 D.3. 4. y N.35 A.6.2. They did during the night. C Coy they occupied their D Coy returned to Bivouac at No. 6 M.1. to take the place in progress of the enemy but unfortunately we were an enemy barrage between the front line & the sunken road. But fortunately are Casualties at intervals throughout the night. There were M.G'S Rifles & also put up a heavy barrage. We evidently expected us to attack.	W.R.
FLERS TRENCHES	18th		Weather very wet.	W.R.
			At intervals throughout the day, the enemy put up two aerial barrages, along the Sunken Rd. But was. During the night of the 18/19th the 5th KING'S OWN relieved the Battalion. We then proceeded to YORK TRENCH which was in a fearful state owing to the heavy rain arriving there at	W.R.
		1.30 A.M.		W.R
			Casualties sustained. 2/Lt. H.R. MANSERGH wounded. M.O.R.KILLED. 11 O.R. wounded & 11 O.R. missing.	W.R
YORK TRENCH	19th		Weather wet.	W.R.
	20th		Batty Resting.	WR.
			Weather fine	WR
POMMIER REDOUBT	21st	8 A.M.	The Battalion proceeded to Bivouac Area at POMMIER REDOUBT. and remained there until the 23.9.16.	WR
	22nd		Weather fine.	W.R.
			Capt. H. AGNEW. R.B.M.C. returned to the 3/1 West Lancs FIELD AMBULANCE, having been relieved by Capt. M°IVOR.	WR.

Army Form C. 2118.

1/9th Batt THE KINGS
(L'pool Regt) T.F.

WAR DIARY or INTELLIGENCE SUMMARY

(Erase heading not required.)

SEPTEMBER 1916

Place	Date	Hour	Summary of Events and Information	Remarks and references to Appendices
POMMIER REDOUBT	23rd		Death etc. The Battn proceeded to the trenches and relieved the 5th KINGS OWN in the front line in N35.a.5.6. dispositions being A Coy on the right & D Coy the left in the front line and B Coy support & C Coy in the reserve cloth shirts. D Coy on the right and B Coy on the left in the 3rd support trench. Battn HQ at N31B57. Bombile D & C 10 P.M. Battn Bombs were collected at N31B57.	10R WLH 1/10000 10R
	24th		The enemy artillery was fairly quiet throughout the day the enemy trench mortars were active. Our bombardment of the enemy lines was fairly accurate & did all day. Our losses incurred through this were very slight. The men & wire shot in considerable quantities were employed in consolidating & improving and advanced trenches. Carrying parties to the junction of parts	10R 10R 10Ro 10R
FLERS TRENCH	25th	At 4:30am	Our bombardment on the 35 Corps line commenced and later on was supplemented by a further increase of bombardment of the enemy's line Strong Points. By now every Army Corps ready for the attack to commence. Orders for which we had received at N35a97. Zero hour was 12:35 P.M. the 35th Corps were detailed to attack on our right and 6th Kings on our right and ANZACS on our left.	10R
		At 12:35 P.M.	Our artillery put up a creeping barrage about 150 yards ahead of our advancing troops. 100 yds between each wave with the Battalion then moved forward in four waves. As the barrage crept forward the men advanced. Battn Bombers on the left of each wave & two parties occupied until the enemy's fortifications almost speechless. A number of Germans surrendered immediately, the remainder were both lay very close up. 175 no losses occurred with a great number of dead & wounded were found dealt with very effectively by our men. A great number of dead by our men. A good deal of our artillery fire gave us some very well. GROVE ALLEY in GROVE ALLEY turned that our artillery (and Corps as 20th) was very weak (C.T. leading to the enemy strong point at N35a97.0-)though there was along way from the enemy's line and reached Seven Dials to Factory Corner Battalion had established Hn of Strong Point Low the Seven Dials 1-5 P.M. 40K or Bomb block at a pt N19 D72. Strong Points being at N19D8.15, N19D8.1, & N19D2.1. They were also in touch with the Regt KINGS on right and the ANZACS on left. A line was established from fresh HQs were moved forward to N20B24. At 4-30 P.M. Battn HQs were moved forward to N20B24. At 4-30 P.M. Battn HQ received an advance of 1000 yds. The 5th KINGS were issued orders to advance from the IRISH avenue at the GROVE ALLEY to be in close support	WLH 1/10000

2449 Wt. W14957/M90. 759,000 1/16 J.B.C. & A. Forms/C.2118/12.

WAR DIARY or INTELLIGENCE SUMMARY

Army Form C. 2118.

19th Battn THE KING'S (L'pool Regt) T.F.

SEPTEMBER 1916

Place	Date	Hour	Summary of Events and Information	Remarks and references to Appendices
FLERS TRENCHES	25th		All available fighting details were organised under 2/Lt RICHER in carrying ammunition & bombs up to the new position and to bring back wounded. This party worked all night & were successful in bringing all wounded in who were lying out. During the night the enemy shelled HQrs front line very heavily.	WR
			Total Casualties sustained from 23/26/9/16	
			KILLED Capt N.L.WATTS. 2/Lt P.W. HANSEN 2/Lt A.J.C.CHALLENER 2/Lt E.G.REDMORE	10R
			Died of wounds. 2/Lt A.R. HENSHIP. Wd 23/9/16	10R
			Wounded. 2/Lt E.W. THOMPSON. 2/Lt T.VICARS. & Major H.K.S.WOODHOUSE	10R
			KILLED 24 Other Ranks	10R
			WOUNDED 136 Other Ranks. MISSING. 15. Other Ranks.	10R
			Capt N.L. WATTS body was removed to the cemetery near POMMIER REDOUBT. the other five bodies were buried near where they fell and crosses were erected.	10R
	26th		During the morning the Battalions whole position including HQs was subjected to an increasing bombardment by the enemy but the actual shells were almost being confined to	10R
		At 8 PM	2 Companies of the 8th IRISH relieved the Battn front being complete at 1-15AM. We then proceeded to YORK TRENCH near GREEN DUMP.	10R
YORK TRENCH	27th			WR
	28th		The Battn proceeded to the Camps at BUIRE-SUR-ANCRE. and remained here until the 1st October.	
BUIRE SUR ANCRE	3rd		A draft of 65 O.R. joined the Battalion as reinforcement	10R
	21st		A draft of 21 O.Rs joined the Battalion as reinforcements	10R

Hugo K.S. Woodhouse
Major
Commanding 19th Kings

CONFIDENTIAL

Vol 18

War Diary

of

1/9th Liverpool Regiment

for the period

1st to 31st October 1916

WAR DIARY or INTELLIGENCE SUMMARY

Army Form C. 2118.

1/9 Batt'n THE KING'S (Liverpool Regt) T.F. Appx No 352

October 1916

Place	Date	Hour	Summary of Events and Information	Remarks and references to Appendices
BURE	1st		Weather fine. 5 Officers and 8 NCOs proceeded to the Trenches at YPRES to take over. Our C.O. received instructions to remain there until the Battalion arrived.	10R
		3.15PM	The Batt'n proceeded to MERICOURT Station and entrained for LONG PRE arriving there at 12 MIDNIGHT. After detraining we marched to COCQUEREL arriving there at 3.15AM. 2½ Out. here they Bivouaced until Reveille at 6.30am.	10R
COCQUEREL	2nd	8.30PM	The Batt'n proceeded to PONT REMY where they entrained for ESQUELBECQ. We arrived at ESQUELBECQ at accompanied by the transport.	10R
WORMHOUDT	3rd	9.30PM	& proceeded to billets at WORMHOUDT. The Batt'n carried out Coy inspections & practical Smoke Helmet Drill. particular attention being paid to men of the new draft.	10R
	4th	12.6PM	The Battalion entrained at WORMHOUDT for POPERINGHE arriving there at 3PM. We marched from until 4PM when we again entrained and proceeded to billets in YPRES returning the 19. Essex Regt. Batt'n HQ's were in the CONVENT.	10R
YPRES	5th		Weather fine. The Battalion proceeded to the Trenches and relieved the 3rd HAMPSHIRES in the front line from ST JEAN I.11.6.8.8. to I.5 & I.3. (ROULERS RAILWAY) exclusive on the night to DURNEST (I.11. R.R.) The 5th KING'S being on our right & the 5th SOUTH LANCS on our left. The dispositions of our Coy in support being "D" Coy on the right in front line, "D" Coy on the left in front line. A Coy in support in X 1 & 2 Trench. "C" Coy with 2 Platoons in X 3 Trench & 2 Platoons in the POTIZZE chateau on the Batt'n Bombers took over the Bombs Posts on the right of the front line in CRATER 6 + K GULLY. Batt'n HQs were in the POTIZZE WOOD. 1st Rd Regt A.D. POST at CHATEAU POTIZE.	ST JEAN sheet 28 sheet 38 10R 16 / 10000
YPRES TRENCHES	6th		Major H.K.S WOOD HOUSE was given the Divisional Commanders authority to wear the badge of Welsh Changate. During the day not enemy was exceptionally quiet.	10R 10R 20R

Army Form C. 2118.

1/8th Battalion THE KING'S (Liverpool Regt.) T.F.

WAR DIARY or INTELLIGENCE SUMMARY
(Erase heading not required.)

October 1916

Place	Date	Hour	Summary of Events and Information	Remarks and references to Appendices
YPRES. TRENCHES. (RAILWAY WOOD SECTOR.)	7th		Weather changeable. WAR was carried out on the trenches, &c:- Owing to the area in which Regiments are situated being so marshy trenches cannot be dug very deep. Numerous breastworks are erected, there as a rule need a considerable amount of labour to keep them in repair, and our men are required to spend the 4 days in billets the present breastworks up in places where they are leaking. The enemy's Artillery has been exceedingly quiet, so M.G's & Trench Mortars are fairly active at night. Our M.G's had news commenced to be active fire.	10 R. 16 R. 10 R.
do	8th		Weather changeable. The enemy's Artillery was a little more active during the morning returns suggesting that the 58 SOUTH LANCS give our all. Our Artillery however co-operated and quietened him. He continued far by desultory fire. Artillery in this sector. A party of 100 men of the 7th KINGS have been sent out to assist us in improving a portion of TRENCH in the extreme right of our line. The trench known as NO 8 CRATER, the ROULERS RAILWAY was fairly shelled during the day at intervals.	10/15 10 R.
do			Lieut. Wayman of the 3rd WEST RIDING Regt. has been attached to the Battalion for instructions in Trench warfare. England got well knocked out throughout the day.	10 R. 10 R.
do	9th		The enemy was very quiet throughout the day. At night enemy M.G's & snipers were fairly active, but any shots were eventually silenced. A party of 7th KINGS (100 men) were sent up to assist in improving the breastwork between G.4.L7 TRENCH, also G.4.L1 TRENCH. This work was started. [Capt. Heath's dugout was shelled men 2/Lt H.L. TYRER 2/Lt J.G. NICHOLLS 2/Lt N. LEES 2/Lt NELSON SMITH slightly wounded]	10 R. 10 R.

WAR DIARY or **INTELLIGENCE SUMMARY**
Army Form C. 2118.

1/9 Batt'n THE KING'S (L'pool Regt) T.F.

— October 1916 — (3)

Place	Date	Hour	Summary of Events and Information	Remarks and references to Appendices
YPRES	10th		Battalion in Trenches. The enemy was very quiet throughout the day.	10/R 40/R
TRENCHES (RAILWAY WOOD SECTOR)		6 P.M.	The 1/9th KING'S relieved the Battalion in the Trenches immediately after which was completed by 8 P.M. One relief party proceeded independently to billets at YPRES. One platoon took over and garrisoned HUSSAR FARM.	60/R
YPRES	11th		During the period the Battalion was in support boy and platoon trainings was carried out. The Battn also supplied a working party of 100 O.R. each night. Boy working on the front line. The Battn remained in support until the night 14/15th.	10/R 10/R
"	13th 14th	11 P.M.	Sgt R.G. WHITE N.R. slight. The Battn relieved by the 1/5 IRISH (L'pool Regt) On relief our boys proceeded independently to the ELVERDINGHE Defences and "L" line relieving the 9/R LANC'S FUSILIERS, the relief was completed by 2.15am on the 15th. Disposition of our boys being B.D.Coys Batt HdQrs & "Shrimp" Redoubt. A Coy in "L" line, Bombers, Snipers & Signal party in the ELVERDINGHE Defences. C Coy had 2 platoons in "L3" & 2 platoons in "L1". Batth HdQrs in "L1".	10/R 10/R
ELVERDINGHE	15th		2/Lt G. CRAWFORD & post were at the CHATEAU at ELVERDINGHE. 2/Lt S.J. HENDRY joined the Battn as reinforcement. The whole of the time the Battn was supplied as follows. The Entrenching Battn 20 O.R. "L" Redoubts R.E.'s 50 O.R. 10's Entrenching Battn 20 O.R. Garrisoned these defences, Box Respirators & Rifles. The remainder of the men carried out platoon & Coy drill.	10/R
"	16	6 P.M. 4.45 P.M.	The enemy shelled Battn HdQrs (the CHATEAU) at the times stated using 5.9 shells. Bullets etc Casualties 1 O.R. 2/Lt D.C.H. FRASER joined the Battn as reinforcements also 12 O.R.'s	10/R 10/R W/R 10/R
"	17th	6 P.M.	The enemy shelled Battn HdQrs (the CHATEAU) at the time stated using 5.9 Shells. 1-2" Shena Point. 4 at 6 P.M. Shelled the CHATEAU 10/R. During the afternoon the enemy shelled "L3" & "L2" killed 3. The following Officers joined the Battn as reinforcements: W.A. TYE, N.L. GELDER, G. TOWLE, C. BASSINGHAM, J.A. MITCHELL, G.F. ROBINSON, A.G. GOWAN, C.B. JOHNSON, C.B. CHILDS, B.S. DAVIES. Casualties 3 O.R.	10/R

2449 Wt. W14957/M90 750,000 1/16 J.B.C. & A. Forms/C.2118/12

WAR DIARY
or
INTELLIGENCE SUMMARY

(Erase heading not required.)

Army Form C. 2118.

1/9 Batt THE KINGS L'pool Regt. T.F.

— OCTOBER 1916 —

Place	Date	Hour	Summary of Events and Information	Remarks and references to Appendices
ELVERDINGHE	18th	11.45pm	The C.O. Commanding reported that patrols of the Battn. killed at ELVERINGHE very quiet but much wiring during evening.	10R.
"	19th	3.15pm	Pilot officer returned from leave. S.E. M. Davis 1st Sth B joined the Batt for duty. Drill was impossible owing to the heavy rain – Lieut-Col replacing	115R.
"	20th	10.15pm	Enemy very quiet during day – first half owing to the weather, heavy day shower later. Wind still dangerous – not S.E. BRUFFELL. In Battn Employed Enemy very quiet – trys of ELVERDINGHE employed in working parties + fatigues	
"	21st		Wind still dangerous. Weather – fine, cold, wind light. Enemy very quiet, but their aeroplanes overhead, vigorously shelled. Training + working parties under R.E. continued	PM
"	22nd		Wind and weather as on 21st. Some artillery duelling in immediate neighbourhood. Schemes of defence for Elverdinghe, and from L2, L8, + L4, submitted to Brigade. Commencing at 4pm the Battalion moved to billets in Ypres. The relief being completed at 9.15pm. The battalion was relieved by the 10th (Scottish) Kings (R'pool Regt) and relieved the	PM
YPRES			9th. (Lnity) Ktr YPRES	
YPRES and	23rd		Wind still dangerous, light S.E. Enemy very quiet. Weather dull, rain at night. Commencing at 5pm. The battalion moved into trenches occupying left Sub-sector of night Brigade. S.S. came trenches as recorded in diary 5th inst. We relieved 2/5 Lancs. Fusiliers. On our right – 1/5 Kings (K'pool)	
YPRES trenches			on our left – 1/5 Kingston (Royal Kane.B.) The disposition of our coys. being: Front line, right, A. Coy. front line, left, C. Coy. In support: D. Coy in X1 + X2 and platoons of B. Coy. in X.3. Polygon defences: B. Coy. less 2platoons. Baths, bombers, Batt. Headquarters and Right dug out as on 5th inst. Relief completed 10.50 pm.	PM
YPRES trenches (RAILWAY WOOD SECTOR)	24th		Very wet all day. Wind dangerous, very light S.E. Enemy very quiet.	PM24

Army Form C. 2118.

WAR DIARY
or
INTELLIGENCE SUMMARY

1/9 Ths King's (Liverpool Regt) T.F.

October 1916

(Erase heading not required.)

Place	Date	Hour	Summary of Events and Information	Remarks and references to Appendices
YPRES Trenches (RAILWAY WOOD SECTOR)	24th		Lt. Col. H.K.S. WOODHOUSE proceeded on leave, & Major R.G.A. LEDERER, MC assumed Temporary command of battalion. Lt. Col. H.H. WAYMAN (West Riding Regt.) Watching over duties of Second in Command attached for instruction.	M
	25th		Wind still dangerous light S.E. Weather dull, and afternoon much of day. Enemy shelled Hike St. & E.end of Haymarket & vicinity, and extent 100-150 yards N. of H.Q. from 11am. to 2 p.m. Estimated no. of shells — 150. Damage, nil. 2/Lt. G.W.C. TRUSCOTT (W. Borders) joined for duty.	M
	26th		Wind dangerous cancelled 7 mind W.N.W. Weather dull, some rain. Enemy shelled Right front Coy. One failed, 1 wounded, all O.R. Defence scheme for L. Battn R. Irish, Rly Way Wood Sector tried by major LEDERER, M.C. to Coy Commdrs. Battn relieved by 7th KINGS at 10.15 PM. Batt. proceeded to billets in YPRES —	M
YPRES	27th		Weather improved. Batth as reinforcement. IV GHG TRUSCOTT joined the Battn as reinforcement.	W.R.
Do	28th		Wind dangerous 10 AM - Church parade for available men - The whole Batt. basked - Reverend SHUREY. Platoon at NUCAR. FARM relieved at 4 PM by platoon of 7th KINGS.	W.R.
Do	29th		2/Lt W.H. GREEN joined the Battn from the 8th Kings.	W.R.
Do			2/Lts G.W.C. TRUSCOTT, G.A. CRAWFORD, B.S. DAVIES, J.C.H. FRASER, C.E. CHILDS, + C. BASSINGHAM proceeded to join the 1st Kings and were struck off the Strength of this Unit. Wind dangerous.	W.R.
Do	30th		Working parties of 150 O.R. were supplied each night whilst the Battn was in YPRES. 2/Lts J.K. EBBELS, S.H. RANDALL, R.H. BORWICK reported joined the Battn as reinforcements.	W.R.
Do	31st		Wind dangerous. Weather showery. The Battn marched to the trenches and relieved the 1st KINGS in the front line. Dispositions of our Coys being the Battn marched to the trenches and relieved the 1st KINGS in the front line. "D" Coy in front line. "C" Coy in Support and "A" & "B" Coys in Reserve - "A" Coy in POTIJZE DEFENCE, "B" in BOYAU + Batth Hqtrs POTIJZE CHATEAU. I.4.9.44.	W.R.

CONFIDENTIAL

Vol 19

War Diary

of

1/9th Liverpool Regt.

for period of

1st November to 30th November 1916

Army Form C. 2118.

WAR DIARY
INTELLIGENCE SUMMARY

1/9th Batt THE KINGS L'pool Regt T.F.

November 1916

Place	Date	Hour	Summary of Events and Information	Remarks and references to Appendices
POTIZZE YPRES (TRENCHES)	1st		Weather fine. Work was carried on repairing trenches, drainage etc.	40R 10R
	2nd		Weather Showery. The enemy shelled Batt Hdqtrs with 3.2, 4.2" Shells. very little damage being done and no casualties sustained. 2nd Lt Tye, C/F Robinson, E. Towle, & J.A. M Tchell were posted and proceeded to join the 13th Kings.	10R 10R 10R
	3rd		Weather Showery. Our Artillery was fairly active through the day. The enemy shelled the front line and C.T. with 77m/m shells but no damage was done.	10R
	4th		Weather Showery.	10R
		11-20pm	The Battn was relieved in the front line by the 4th Kings. On completion of relief, the Battn proceeded to Brielen by Y PRES with the exception of 300 O.R. who proceeded to Hull respective findugrous for working parties. The enemy was very quiet throughout the relief.	20R 10R
YPRES.	5th		Weather Showery. Lt Col HKS Woodhouse returned from leave and assumed command of the Battalion. Major O. Ledgers R.F.A. taking over second in command	20R 10R
	6th		A working party of 100 O.R. was supplied for cable burying under R.E.	20R 10R
			Weather Showery. Platoon & Coy drill was carried out. Working parties numbering 327 O.R. were supplied by the Unit for working on Cambridge Junct. Cable burying & carrying parties.	20R 10R
	7th		Enemy shelled the Clock Hall during the morning. Weather Showery. Platoon Coy Brill + Box Respirator drill carried out. The Battn was relieved in YPRES by the 1/8th IRISH and proceeded by train to Brandhoek & thence to "B" Camp. (G.b.d. 4.2) arriving there at 10-30pm.	20R 10R 10R 10R
"B" Camp G.b.d. 4.2.	8th		Weather fine. Coy training carried out.	40R 10R
	9th		Weather fine. Coy training carried out. Arms drill close order and extended order drill.	10R 10R 20R

Army Form C.2118.

WAR DIARY
or
INTELLIGENCE SUMMARY.
(Erase heading not required.)

1/9 Batt "The King's" Liverpool Regt.
T.F.

November 1916

Place	Date	Hour	Summary of Events and Information	Remarks and references to Appendices
"B" Camp G6d 4.2.	10th		Weather fine. Coy training carried out, & the Battn was inspected by the Commanding Officer	
	11th		Weather fine. Coy training carried out and Battn was bathed & received clean underclothing	
	12th		Weather fine. Coy training during the morning, and Church Parade during the afternoon	
	13th		Weather showery. The Battn supplied a working party of 300 O.R. for Cable Burying	
	14th		Weather fine. At a ceremonial parade held at Bde Hdqrs the following NCOs received decorations:— Sergt EDINGTON, MUNCASTER, ₂/₀ JONES M.S.M.; Sergt CHISNALL, Corpl DENTLEY, Sgll HILTON M.M. & Sergt CHISNALL, Medal of St. GEORGE 2nd Class (Russian).	
	15th		Weather fine. Coy training carried out & the Battn and Box Respirators fitted by Divisional Gas Officer. & was put through Gas.	
	16th		Weather fine. Coy training carried out.	

Army Form C. 2118.

WAR DIARY
or
INTELLIGENCE SUMMARY.
(Erase heading not required.)

1/9 Batt"y "THE KINGS" Liverpool Regt T.F.

NOVEMBER 1916

Place	Date	Hour	Summary of Events and Information	Remarks and references to Appendices
B' Camp G ba n 3.	17th		Weather Showery. Coy training carried out. Whilst the Brigade was in Divisional reserve Classes were carried on to instruct Junior Officers under Bde Major; Senr NCOs under Staff Capt; Lecture to Officers by Brigadier General & Col. Fairclough, Bombing, and Lewis Gun Classes under Brigade and Battalion arrangements. All Battalion Bombers had practice in wire Destruction & also 6 Bombers per Coy.	10R 10R
	19th		Weather wet. During the morning Coys practices diving.	10R 10R 10R
		8 PM	The Bn entrained at BRANDHOEK for YPRES arriving there at 6 PM and marching to relieve the 1st KINGS in Dwgs in YPRES. the relief was completed by 8 PM.	10R 10R 10R
YPRES.	19		157. O.R. joined the Battalion as reinforcements. Weather fine. The Battln supplied working parties of 357. O.R. each day while in YPRES. The weather Dull, wet. were carried out & also Arms Drill. 6. O.R. joined Battalion as reinforcements.	10R 10R 10R 10R 10R

Army Form C. 2118.

WAR DIARY or INTELLIGENCE SUMMARY.

1/9 Batt" THE KINGS. Liverpool Regt. T.F.

NOVEMBER 1916

Place	Date	Hour	Summary of Events and Information	Remarks and references to Appendices
YPRES.	20th		Weather fine.	P.O
	21st		Arms Drill and musketry carried out, also working parties supplied. Weather fine	P.O
	22nd		Platoon drill etc carried out, also working parties supplied. Weather Dull	P.O
	23rd		Platoon Drill & Box Respirator Drill carried out. Working parties supplied.	P.O
	24th		The Batt relieved the 7th Kings in the trenches. relief carried out successfully by 9 pm	P.O
	25th		Weather Dull	P.O
	26th		Weather Wet.	P.O
	27th		Weather fine	P.O
			Heavy bombardment by enemy trench mortars for 1 hour, no casualties	P.O
			Weather fine.	P.O
	28th		Some hostile shelling	P.O
			Should have been relieved by 7th Kings but relief was postponed on a/c of a raid to be carried out by 6th Kings on our right. Raid cancelled.	P.O
	29th		Relief again cancelled. Raid took place & was very successful.	P.O
	30		Relieved by 7th Kings and Batt supplied 10 G.O.P for working parties. Returned to billets in YPRES	P.O

Vol 20

CONFIDENTIAL

War Diary
of
19th Liverpool Regt.
for period
December 1st - 31st 1916

No 759

1/9th Batn "The Kings" Army Form C. 2118.
(L'pool Regt.) T.F

WAR DIARY

INTELLIGENCE SUMMARY

DECEMBER 1916

Place	Date	Hour	Summary of Events and Information	Remarks and references to Appendices
YPRES	1st		Weather fine	
			Batt. came into billets during the night and devoted the day to cleaning up and inspection	P.D
"	2nd		Weather fine	
			Batt supplied 250 O.R for working parties remainder under Coy officers for training	P.D
"	3rd		Weather fine	
			250 O.R for working parties. Church parades for remainder in the morning. Bathing in the afternoon at Brigade baths. There was a voluntary Church Parade at 6.30 in the evening also Holy Communion was administered at 11.45 a.m	P.D
"	4th		Batt paraded to Command Square for the Commanding Officer to present cards signed by the Div Commander to officers and O.R men recommended for gallantry on the Somme. Batt also supplied working parties.	P.D
"	5th		Weather wet	
			Batt relieved 4th The Kings during the afternoon and night in the L Sub section of the Brigade front. The relief was carried out successfully	P.D
"	6th		Weather fine	
			Some enemy trench mortar activity on our right front Coy trenches. 2 Casualties (1 killed in dugout, 1 wounded, not seriously)	P.D

Army Form C. 2118.

WAR DIARY
or
INTELLIGENCE SUMMARY.
(Erase heading not required.)

Instructions regarding War Diaries and Intelligence Summaries are contained in F. S. Regs., Part II. and the Staff Manual respectively. Title pages will be prepared in manuscript.

Place	Date	Hour	Summary of Events and Information	Remarks and references to Appendices
	7th		Weather fine	
	8th		One O.R. killed by enemy aircraft. Major Welchin assumes Command. Capt & Lt Perry rejoin Batt. as reinforcements after having been struck off the strength & again taken on the strength. Weather fine	QD
	9th		The Batt. was relieved in the L Sub district by 2/5 Lancs Fusiliers ___ entrained at YPRES for BRANDHOEK and billeted in B Camp. Relief was carried out successfully. Weather fine	RD
	10th		The day was spent in inspections by Coy Commanders and bathing the men. Weather fine	QD
	11th		Church parade in the morning, not much in the afternoon. Weather fine	Q
	12th		The Batt. was inspected by Coy by the Commanding officer. Coy's when not being inspected carried musketry from the 30 yds rifle range. Weather very wet in the early morning afterwards a cover of snow. The day was spent in lectures by Coy officers	RD QD

T2134. Wt. W708—776. 500000. 4/15. Sir J. C. & S.

Army Form C. 2118.

WAR DIARY
or
INTELLIGENCE SUMMARY.
(Erase heading not required.)

Instructions regarding War Diaries and Intelligence Summaries are contained in F. S. Regs., Part II. and the Staff Manual respectively. Title pages will be prepared in manuscript.

Place	Date	Hour	Summary of Events and Information	Remarks and references to Appendices
B. Camps	13th		Weather fine	10 R.
"	14th		Baths & Games carried out.	10 R.
			Weather showery	10 R.
"	15th		Coy. & Bttn. drainning carried out, particulars attached being sent to Musketry	10 R.
			Weather fine	10 R.
			Coy drainning carried out during the morning. Gas alarm carried out in the afternoon. The Battn. marched past the Major Gen. at EDWARD'HOEK	10 R.
				10 R.
	15th		Bttn. drainning carried out. 10 R.	10 R.
				10 R.
"	16th		Loosehetn	10 R.
			Working party of 100 men supplied for Cable burying. Distribution of ribbons by Lt. Major Gen. during afternoon to the following No. 2418 Pte OTTY. No.3052 Pte BUXTON. No.2915 Pte ANDERSON. Military Medals. An experiment was also carried out, constructing trenches by explosion.	
			Weather fine	10 R.
	M th		The Battn. entrained at TRANDHOEK at 4 P.M. and proceeded to billets at YPRES arriving there at 6.15pm and relieved Rx. 2/5 LANCS BAS.	10 R.
				10 R.
				10 R.

Army Form C. 2118.

WAR DIARY
or
INTELLIGENCE SUMMARY.
(Erase heading not required.)

Instructions regarding War Diaries and Intelligence Summaries are contained in F. S. Regs., Part II. and the Staff Manual respectively. Title pages will be prepared in manuscript.

Place	Date	Hour	Summary of Events and Information	Remarks and references to Appendices
YPRES.	19th		Another fine day. Coy training carried out during the morning. The Batt: proceeded to Reinforce and relieve the 1/8 IRISH (Irish Regt) on the front line, being the ROULERS YPRES Railway and Rgt being KOYLI HAYMARKET, 2 & 5th Kings were on our right. The LN'Lans on our left. If dispositions of our Coys being A Coy on the right in front line, C Coy in R of A in support. D Coy in Ry Cutting and B Coy g Watsons left support + 2 platoons on POTIJZE DEFENSE.	
"	19th		Roads wet. Enemy very quiet.	
"	20.		Weather fine at first, then dense mist. Lieut. & Adjt. W. Reins having been attached to Brigade for instructions as from today 2/Lieut. G.G. Maurice took over duties of Acting Adjt. The enemy shewed some artillery & trench mortar activity, mainly about 11am. and 4.30pm. about 38. H.E. and 38 77pm attaching trenches neighbourhood of our front line, PICCADILLY, GULLY + CAMBRIDGE trenches, also	DM

DECEMBER 1916

4/4th Battn "The King's"
(L'pool Regt)

WAR DIARY or INTELLIGENCE SUMMARY.
Army Form C. 2118.

Place	Date	Hour	Summary of Events and Information	Remarks and references to Appendices
YPRES				
Con'd	20th		On ROILERS Rly. HELLFIRE CORNER T2. About 23 T.M. bombs were also dropped. Very little damage was done on our lines.	M
	21st		Weather wet, high wind at night. CAMBRIDGE Trench & PICCADILLY were heavily shelled morning & afternoon, the trenches being blown in in several places. Casualties: 1 killed, 5 wounded.	M
	22nd		Weather changeable, dampish work. WIND SAFE. Artillery on both sides again very active, our left front & front end of HAYMARKET C.T. being especially heavily shelled, C. Coy H.Q. & cooker being hit. No casualties. The battalion was relieved in the trenches by the 7th. King's (L'pool Regt) relief being complete at 8.45 p.m. The battalion taking over billets in YPRES from the 7th King's.	M
	23rd		In the absence of Lt. Colonel H.K.S. WOODHOUSE on leave Major J.E.B. LEWIS 18th as shown 14th inst. Cmmdg. ROYAL WELSH FUSILIERS assumed duties of 2nd in Command vice Major PRAUSSERER M.C. Commanding. Training; Amusements; Bon Rapports Mill. Cleaning up. Working Parties.	M
	24th		Weather dry, gale morning. Considerable fall of snow & some hail fell, making the ½ hour march to Café dim Pither. Working Parties. Bomb-proof finish to filling in cellar. Peaceful fire. Training: Bombers; musketry; drill. Camp fatigues. Dull. Wiring restored. Divine services.	M

Army Form C. 2118.

1/19th Battn The Kings Lpool Regt

WAR DIARY
or
INTELLIGENCE SUMMARY.

DECEMBER 1916

(Erase heading not required.)

Instructions regarding War Diaries and Intelligence Summaries are contained in F. S. Regs., Part II. and the Staff Manual respectively. Title pages will be prepared in manuscript.

Place	Date	Hour	Summary of Events and Information	Remarks and references to Appendices
YPRES	25th		Weather wet. Various working parties, Christmas greetings were received from the Army Corps, Divisional & Brigade Commanders.	Apk
	26th		Weather fine. The men had their Xmas dinners in a church in YPRES. Christmas greetings were received from His Majesty the King, Lord Derby, His Majesty the King of the Belgians.	Apk
	27th		Weather fine. High wind. Training dangerous. 1 hour Musketry. 1 hour Box Respirator (Q will Physical training. 1 hour Musketry. 1 hour Box Respirator). Battn. bathed at A.W.L. baths. The battalion relieved the 1st Kings (Lpool Regt) in the left sector of the brigade. "B" Coy Right front, "D" Coy left front, "A" Coy Right support, "C" Coy left support. The relief was carried out successfully.	Apk Apk

Army Form C. 2118.

WAR DIARY
or
INTELLIGENCE SUMMARY.
(Erase heading not required.)

9th Bn The King's Liverpool Regt

Instructions regarding War Diaries and Intelligence December 1916
Summaries are contained in F.S. Regs., Part II.
and the Staff Manual respectively. Title pages
will be prepared in manuscript.

Place	Date	Hour	Summary of Events and Information	Remarks and references to Appendices
YPRES.	28TH		Weather changeable. Our line was heavily shelled between 1 & 2 pm, but very little damage was done. Casualties. Nil.	BELGIUM SHEET. 28 NW EDITION 4A 1/10,000
	29th		Weather very wet. WIND: SAFE. Fairly Strong. HAYMARKET & PICCADILLY Communication trenches were flooded in places as deep as 18 inches. Casualties. Nil.	Our
	30TH		During the temporary absence of Major T.G.A. LEDERER M.C. on course, Major J.E. LEWIS of 15th Bn Royal Welsh Fusiliers assumed command of this Bn. Weather fine. Slight wind. Some enemy T.M. & artillery activity on our front & support trenches in direction of YPRES. Casualties. Nil.	Our
	31ST		Weather fine but dull. Enemy artillery active on our front line & YPRES. Machine guns of enemy more active than usual. Casualties. 2nd Lieut Rawle WOUNDED. Other Ranks [illegible]	Our

S.M 21

165/55

War Diary
of the
1/9th Liverpool R.
for the period
1/1/7 to 31/1/7.

WAR DIARY
or
INTELLIGENCE SUMMARY.

Army Form C. 2118.

9th Bn The King's Liverpool Regiment

Place	Date	Hour	Summary of Events and Information	Remarks and references to Appendices
YPRES	1ST		Weather fine. Orders were received that a bombardment of enemy trenches would take place at 5:30 (ZERO) pm by our artillery. We cleared our front line trenches at 4:30pm and at 5:30 pm our artillery, Stokes mortars & trench mortars opened up "Box" style of bombardment which started firing on two points about 80x apart and gradually closed in. Considerable damage was done to enemy trenches. Almost immediately after our artillery started the Boshe sent up green flares which were answered with two stars + in five minutes the enemy artillery put up a slow barrage on our front line i.e. front line communication trenches + support line. The bombardment lasted for about 20 minutes ceasing at 5:50 pm. We then sent forward party	BELGIUM SHEET 2 B in EDITION 1A / 20,000

Army Form C. 2118.

WAR DIARY
or
INTELLIGENCE SUMMARY.
(Erase heading not required.)

9th Bn. the Kings Liverpool Regiment

JANUARY 1917

Place	Date	Hour	Summary of Events and Information	Remarks and references to Appendices
YPRES	1st		Comp. patrols out the communication trenches to ascertain the situation. On their return they reported no resistance to the three levels, saw Posts left, there in charge of an officer, but the damage done to that part of the line occupied by the left front Company was fairly severe, it being knocked in in several places & the parapet was not sufficiently high to give cover from view. HAYMARKET has blown in in 5 places over PICCADILLY was badly knocked about, the first 20 yards being almost impassable. The situation had completely pictured losing 6.30 p.m. the order was thus given to reoccupy the front line, this being carried out in the most successful manner.	

Army Form C. 2118.

WAR, DIARY
or
INTELLIGENCE SUMMARY.
(Erase heading not required.)

9th Bn The King's
Liverpool Regiment

Place	Date	Hour	Summary of Events and Information	Remarks and references to Appendices
YPRES	1st	CONTD	Our men then started to work to repair the damage and, after working all night, by "stand to" at 6.30 am HAYMARKET & PICCADILLY were completely cleared of all debris repaired, the front line was also cleared repaired, and altogether some very excellent work was done. During the whole of the bombardment & retaliation we had no casualties. CASUALTIES Other Ranks 1 KILLED. 1 WOUNDED.	
	2nd		Weather fine until evening, when it rained very heavily. The Battalion was relieved by the 1st Kings then Companies commencing soon after dark. Relief was carried out successfully & complete by 7.0 pm. The Brigadier went round the trenches in the morning & was very pleased with the work done by our men, in consequence, orders which	

Army Form C. 2118.

WAR DIARY
or
INTELLIGENCE SUMMARY.
(Erase heading not required.)

9th The King's
Liverpool Regiment

Place	Date	Hour	Summary of Events and Information	Remarks and references to Appendices
YPRES	2nd	Cont'd	We had four large working parties were cancelled. We took over the same billets in YPRES.	Aug.
	3rd		Weather changeable. The day was spent in cleaning equipment etc. Drills ½ hour Box Respirator Drill. ¾ hour Physical Drill. Various working parties.	
			1 hour London Gazette 31/11/16 — 2nd Lieut. H.K.S. WOODHOUSE = Appointed a Companion of the Distinguished Service Order (Temp'y)	Cont'd July
	4th		Weather fine. Parades. 1 hour Physical Training, 1½ hours Musketry. Afternoon, Inspection of equipment etc. Various working parties.	Aug.
	5th		Weather fine. The enemy shelled YPRES in the vicinity of the square, about 250 H.E. & S.9 falling. Drill:- 1 hr's Bayonet fighting, 1½ hours Musketry. 1 hr's Box Respirator Drill.	
			CASUALTIES. 1 KILLED, 1 WOUNDED, 4 WOUNDED but at duty. All OTHER RANKS	July

Army Form C. 2118.

9th The King's
Liverpool Regiment

WAR DIARY
or
INTELLIGENCE SUMMARY.
(Erase heading not required.)

JANUARY 1917

Place	Date	Hour	Summary of Events and Information	Remarks and references to Appendices
YPRES	6th		Weather fine. The enemy did very little shelling during day by lit out about 5:0pm when the transport arrived. The town was lightly shelled. We were relieved in the billets in YPRES by the 2/5 LANCS. FUS. They arrived about 5:15 pm + the relief was complete by 6pm. Our battalion then proceeded to the tramway en route for "C" Camp. We detrained at BRANDHOEK and after a 45 minutes march we arrived at the camp. CASUALTIES. 1 other rank WOUNDED	
	7th		Weather fine. Lieut & Adjutant W. Raine + No 1027 C.S.M. Ash (wounded 25/9/16) are both awarded the Military Cross. Mentioned in dispatches:- Capt (temp Lt Col) H.K.S. WOODHOUSE D.S.O. Capt (temp Major) A.W. FULTON (Killed 17.8.16) Capt (temp Major) N.L. WATTS (Killed 25.9.16) Lieut (temp Major)	

Army Form C. 2118.

WAR DIARY
or
INTELLIGENCE SUMMARY.
(Erase heading not required.)

9th The King's Liverpool Regt.

Place	Date	Hour	Summary of Events and Information	Remarks and references to Appendices
YPRES	7th	CONTD	(Lieut (temp Capt) W.K. PERRY, No 2967 Pte A. BOWYER B.Co. of The day was spent in CHURCH PARADES & cleaning up. Weather fine.	Aug
	8th		Major P.G.A. LEDERER, M.C. having returned resumed command of the Battalion today. Parades 9 hrs Running drill, 1½ hrs Platoon drill with arms, 1½ hrs Musketry. In tomorrow - games. Weather changeable.	Aug 7
	9th		Parades 9 hrs Running drill, Inspections. 12 other rank reinforcements arrived. Weather changeable.	Aug
	10th		Its a very long party was detailed with a guide from the R.E. it was impossible for any Jetvill, Lewis gunners went firing down the range. L. Cpl. DUNN of PHILADELPHIA having sent a cheque to the King	Aug

Army Form C. 2118.

9th The King's
[?] Regt

WAR DIARY
or
INTELLIGENCE SUMMARY.

January 1917

(Erase heading not required.)

Place	Date	Hour	Summary of Events and Information	Remarks and references to Appendices
YPRES 10th Camp CORPS in POPERINGHE	11th		The BATTN will be able to go to the DIVL THEATRE. Weather changeable. Lt.Col H.K.S. WOODHOUSE having resumed command as from the 10th inst. PARADES. 4 hrs + Saluting drill Inspection of Box Respirators Demonstration in use of rockets as S.O.S. Signal MAJOR. J.E. LEWIS, 18th ROYAL WELSH FUSILIERS (attacked this unit) will assume command (temply) of 7th The KINGS from tomorrow 12th inst	Cinile Anglo
	12th		Weather dull. Large party supplied, to be met at VLAMERTINGHE CHURCH by R.E.	
	13th	1/am – 3/pm	Weather – heavy rain Battalion moved from C CAMP to Z CAMP (F.25.c 8.1 Map 27 1/40,000)	JE

Army Form C. 2118.

WAR DIARY
or
INTELLIGENCE SUMMARY.
(Erase heading not required.)

9TH THE KING'S LIVERPOOL REGIMENT

JANUARY 1917

Place	Date	Hour	Summary of Events and Information	Remarks and references to Appendices
Z CAMP (ST. JAHN-TER-BIEZEN)	14th		Half an inch of snow, clear later. CHURCH PARADE and cleaning of Camp. 2/LIEUT. BARKER, H.B.M., 2/LIEUT. JENKINSON H.W., 2/LIEUT. GREEVES N.M., drafted to the Battalion.	
"	15th		Draft of 90 Other Ranks for the 7TH KING'S attached to the 9TH KING'S temporarily. Slight frost. Platoon and Company training.	
"	16th	3.30 pm	Lecture to Officers and N.C.Os by BRIG.-GEN. F.J DUNCAN C.M.G, D.S.O. Weather frosty. Company training. Lecture to Officers by LT-COL. H.K.S. WOODHOUSE. D.S.O. Returned from hospital CAPT ATKINSON. F. Draft of 34 Other Ranks (untrained) arrived for 9TH KING'S.	
"	17th		Draft of 50 Other Ranks for 7TH KING'S attached to the 9TH KING'S temporarily. Heavy snow all day. Draft of 7 Other Ranks for 7TH KING'S attached to the 9TH KING'S temporarily. Draft of 70 Other Ranks (untrained) for the 9TH KING'S arrived.	
"	18th		Snow and rain, freezing later. Company training, including range practice.	
"	19th	5 pm	Lecture to Officers by BRIG.-GEN. F.J DUNCAN C.M.G., D.S.O. Snow, freezing at dusk. Company training; making strong points and attack from trenches. Night Outpost scheme.	
"	20th	11 am	Inspection of new drafts by BRIG.-GEN. F.J. DUNCAN C.M.G., DSO. Frost, three inches of snow lying. Company training & football. New drafts inspected by Divisional Gas Officer.	

Army Form C. 2118.

WAR DIARY
or
INTELLIGENCE SUMMARY.

(Erase heading not required.)

9TH THE KING'S LIVERPOOL REGIMENT

JANUARY 1917

Place	Date	Hour	Summary of Events and Information	Remarks and references to Appendices
Z. CAMP	21st		Hard frost: three inches of snow lying and all water pipes frozen. CHURCH PARADE. Drafts of 5TH & 6TH KING'S attached to 9TH KING'S till 22nd inst., on 6TH KING'S leaving Y Camp	A/2
JAHN-TER-BIEZEN	22nd		Frost continued. Parades – Baths, Company training; lecture to Officers by Lt.-Col. WOODHOUSE D.S.O. & MAJ. GEN. LEDERER M.C.	A/2
"	23rd		All new drafts (including 5TH, 6TH and 7TH KING'S attached) proceeded to new Reinforcement Camp (X camp). Frost continued. Company training: attack under dummy Trench Mortar barrage; night marching and patrolling.	A/2
"	24th		Frost continued. Battalion training: attack from trenches and consolidation of position: GENL. SIR HERBERT C.O. PLUMER G.C.M.G., K.C.B., MAJ.-GENL. A.S. JEUDWINE C.B. and BRIG.-GEN. F.J. DUNCAN, C.M.G., D.S.O. present. Afternoon – games. Lecture to Officers by MAJ. GEN. LEDERER M.C.	A/2
"	25th		Frost continued. Battalion training: Advance Guard practice to HOUTKERQUES. Lecture to Subalterns, C.S.M's, + Sergts, on "Discipline" by 2/Lt. F.J. MAURICE. Evening: night Assembly	M
"	26th		Practice + march. Major P.G.A. LEDERER proceeded to viii Corps for attachment to Q" branch. Frost continued. Battalion training: Outpost Scheme.	M
"	27th		Frost continued, Battalion training; Assembly practice. Afternoon – Games.	M
"	28th		Frost continued. (Sunday) Inspection of Lewis Gun teams with unorganised transport, also of horses feet equipment + kit inspection; practice in fitting equipment made by Brig. Gen. F.J. DUNCAN, C.M.G. A S.O. in accordance with G.H.Q. pamphlet.	M

Army Form C. 2118.

WAR DIARY
or
INTELLIGENCE SUMMARY.
(Erase heading not required.)

Instructions regarding War Diaries and Intelligence Summaries are contained in F.S. Regs., Part II. and the Staff Manual respectively. Title pages will be prepared in manuscript.

Place	Date	Hour	Summary of Events and Information	Remarks and references to Appendices
T Camps, ST. JAN-TER-BIEZEN.	29th		Rest continued. The 9th King's relieved this unit as T Camps, the 9th King's marching to PROVEN where it took over billets. Lieut RICHER, L.R.S. proceeded, with 17 other ranks, to take command of pour detachment at BERTHES.	Bn
and PROVEN				
PROVEN	30th		Rest continued. Battalion paraded for work on Railway construction.	Bn
"	31st		" " " Lewis Gun classes for all officers formed under 2/Lt. R.C. WILDE and C.B. JOHNSON to be held each day from 9.30 a.m. to 12.30 p.m. Daily classes under Lt. Col. H.K.S. WOODHOUSE, D.S.O. Cmdg on "Training" Division for Offensive action, were started, to be held from 5.30 to 6.30 p.m.	Bn

Ingot Monstone
Lieut. Colonel Commanding
9th The King's.

T2134. Wt. W708—776. 500000. 4/15. Sir J. C. & S.

CONFIDENTIAL.

War Diary

of

1/9th Liverpool Regt

for the period

1st to 28th February 1917

Army Form C. 2118.

WAR DIARY
or
INTELLIGENCE SUMMARY.

9th Bn. THE KINGS (LPh. REGT) TF

February 1917

Place	Date	Hour	Summary of Events and Information	Remarks and references to Appendices
PROVEN	1st		Frost continued. Battalion on Railway Construction with Capt. J.H. HALLIWELL	
	2nd		Proceeded to ROYAL FLYING CORPS.	
	3rd		Frost continued, Battn. on Rly. Constrn. work	
	4th		Ditto	
	5th		" "	
	6th		" "	
	7th		" "	
	8th		" "	
	9th		" "	
	10th		" "	
	11th		" "	One Case Scarlet fever notified	
	12th		" "	Second " " "	
	13th		" "	
	14th		" "	
	15th		" "	

Army Form C. 2118.

WAR DIARY
or
INTELLIGENCE SUMMARY.
(Erase heading not required.)

Instructions regarding War Diaries and Intelligence Summaries are contained in F. S. Regs., Part II. and the Staff Manual respectively. Title pages will be prepared in manuscript.

9th. Bn. THE KING'S (L'P'L. REGT.)

February 1917

Place	Date	Hour	Summary of Events and Information	Remarks and references to Appendices
PROVEN	16th		Bn on Railway Construction Work. 2 cases German measles	M
	17th		Work continued. Ditto	M
	18th		Work continued. Ditto 3rd Case German measles.	M
	19th		Work continued. Ditto 4th " "	M
	20th		Work continued. Ditto 5th " "	M
	21st		Work continued. Ditto 6th " "	M
	22nd		Ditto "	M
PROVEN and YPRES	23rd		Bn on Railway Contin. work. The battalion moved into billets at the Prison.	M
YPRES RAILWOOD SECTOR	24th		YPRES, entraining at PROVEN at 5.30 p.m. and detraining at ASYLUM, YPRES. Men'd Safe. The battalion moved into left sub-sector of Right Brigade sector, the disposition of Companies being; Right Front — A. Coy. Left Front — B. Coy. Right Support — C. Coy. Left Support — D. Coy. Lt Col. H.K.S. WOODHOUSE D.S.O. to England.	M
	25th		Wind N.W. Fine. Partly bright. Evening. Slight artillery activity.	Lt Col. STANDAGE (Major RE) assumed command of the battalion vice Lt Col. H.K.S. WOODHOUSE DSO to England	M
	26th		" " " " " " " one man killed two slightly wounded.	M
	27th		" " " " " Shyes artillery activity.	Nil.
	28th		" " " " " Moderate artillery activity.	M
	29th		Rations frontage reduced on night 28/29 commencing at I.5.3 incl. and widened on left north at 0.29.3 inclusive.	M

J. M. Dunn Lieut. Col.
Commanding, 1/8th Batt. "THE KING'S"

Army Form C. 2118.

WAR DIARY
or
INTELLIGENCE SUMMARY.   1/5 THE KING'S (L'POL. REGT.) T.F.
(Erase heading not required.)

Instructions regarding War Diaries and Intelligence Summaries are contained in F.S. Regs., Part II. and the Staff Manual respectively. Title pages will be prepared in manuscript.

Month: March 1917

Place	Date	Hour	Summary of Events and Information	Remarks and references to Appendices
YPRES RAILWAY WOOD SECTOR	1st		Wind dangerous. Enemy TM'y very active throughout. Some aeroplane activity on both sides. At 11.30 p.m. we blew a small mine to immediate East of No 3 crater, under enemy front line. Intense bombardment by our artillery followed at fixed intervals. A patrol sent out by this unit, having enemy trap head into No 5 crater, no objective lost. 1 man killed. Stretcher bearers showed a hit.	PM
	2nd		Wind dangerous. ~~TM activity~~ Enemy TM'y very active. Generally quiet day.	AM
			" Misty night throughout. Enemy's snipers especially active. Slight artillery activity.	PM
	3rd		Cold + dull. Misty night throughout.	AM
			The Battalion was relieved by the 2/K. King's (K'pl. Reg't) and moved into billets	PM
YPRES	4th		in YPRES. Wind dangerous. Chiefly snowy, Inspection ~~training~~ + lectures. At night a raid was carried out on enemy trap adjoining No.5 Crater. Two German prisoners were captured by the fighting patrol under 2/Lt. Wilde. 9/Lt. Wilde + 2/Lt. Elam received command of enemy posts. Lieut Hardy directed operations from front line trench. Casualties: Lt. R. Darling wounded, 2/Lt. R.C. Willis slightly wounded, 1 man killed, 4 wounded, 1 missing.	PM
	5th		3½ hours bombing raid. Two Drilly Peachers ran wingsford fighting over. Bathing parties by companies. A patrol sent out by this unit to pts. area missing from last night's patrol was unable to find any trace of him.	ULS

T3134. Wt. W708—776. 500000. 4/16. Sir J. C. & S.

WAR DIARY or INTELLIGENCE SUMMARY

Army Form C. 2118.

1/9 THE KINGS (L'POOL. REGT.) T.F.

Month: March 1917.

Place	Date	Hour	Summary of Events and Information	Remarks and references to Appendices
YPRES.	6th		3½ hours Platoon Training including Anti Gas Drill & Battery of Fives & fatigue order. Working parties.	CEL
BRANDHOEK "C" Camp.	7th		Battalion relieved in Ypres by 10th K.L.R. & moved to "C" Camp by train to BRANDHOEK	CEL
	8th		Inspections & Cleaning up. 3½ hours Organised Games in afternoon	CEL
			Platoon & Company drill 4 hours. Afternoon 1 Coy on Range, 1 Coy Inspection, 1 Coy Instruction in Guards. Specialists own Training. 1st Lectures to Officers & N.C.O. by C.O. & R.S.M. respectively	CEL CEL
	9th		Company Battery parades in turn	
			Platoon & Company drill, including Anti Gas Drill 4 hours. Afternoon 1 Coy on Range. 1 Coy Inspection. 1 Coy Instruction in Guards. 1 Coy digging Strong. Specialists own training. Lectures to Officers by C.O.	CEL
	10th		Lecture to N.C.O.s by R.S.M. 1 hour test.	CEL
	11th		New numbers given to O.R.s (A.C.I. 2414, 1916). 4 hours Bn'ly Route March. Organised Games in afternoon	CEL
	12th		Church Parade. Battalion inspection by C.O.	CEL
			Coys re-organised on new basis i.e. 1 Section L.G., 1 Section Rifles & 1 Section Rifles & Rifle Grenades	
			His Drill & Coys in attack from trench to trench (4 hours). Afternoon 1 Coy on Range, 1 Coy Instruction in Guards, & 2 Coys digging Strong Point. Specialists own training.	CEL
	13th		2nd Anniversary of Ninth arrival in France. 4 hours Drill by Coys on attack from trench to trench.	CEL
			Coys re-organised on new basis, as on the 12th.	CEL

Army Form C. 2118.

WAR DIARY
or
INTELLIGENCE SUMMARY.
(Erase heading not required.)

1/9 THE KINGS (L'POOL REGT.) T.F.

MARCH 1917.

Place	Date	Hour	Summary of Events and Information	Remarks and references to Appendices
BRANDHOEK "C" CAMP	14th		Drill & all ranks passed through Gas Chamber, 4 hours. 1 Coy on Range other Coys organised Games	CHEK
	15th		Inspection by the Brigadier of the brigade who spoke to Major & B.T.J. PERRY with the M.C. ribbon & L/Cpl McREED with the Croix de Guerre ribbon. The Brigade then marched past the Brigadier. Brigade sports were held in the afternoon the most winning the footballmatch against the 11 K.R.R., the Rifle Grenade Competition and second in the Bomb throwing.	
	16th		Drill & temperes in the attack from trench to trench. 4 hours "C" Camp were taken over by the 4th King's Own whilst this unit took over from the 10th K.R.R. in YPRES	CEL
YPRES	17th		proceeding thereby from BRANDHOEK. Weather fine & clear. Heavy hostile shelling of YPRES. Casualties nothing unit, 1 killed, 3 wounded, of which one died since. The Battalion relieved the 1/5th Royal North Lancs Regt. in the left subsector.	M...
YPRES RAILWAY WOOD SECTOR.	18th		Wind safe. Weather fine. Enemy artillery active on front lines. Patrol of 1 Off. 20 OR wounded	
	19th		otherwise reports generally weak. 2Lt R.C.WILDE & 2Lt R.C.H. ELLAM awarded the MILITARY CROSS	
	20th		Weather dull. Wind safe. Enemy raided our left hand Coy by a hopper. OR killed, 9 wounded, 13 missing. Time 4.40 a.m. A Patrol found 8 Ger. in open with a dead German N.F.Co. Ellval Servel wound. 1. O.R. Wind dangerous died all day. 1 O.R. General Service wound. Enemy artillery quiet	

Army Form C. 2118.

WAR DIARY
or
INTELLIGENCE SUMMARY.

MARCH 1917.   1/9 THE KINGS (L'POOL REGT.) T.F.

(Erase heading not required.)

Instructions regarding War Diaries and Intelligence Summaries are contained in F. S. Regs., Part II. and the Staff Manual respectively. Title pages will be prepared in manuscript.

Place	Date	Hour	Summary of Events and Information	Remarks and references to Appendices
YPRES RAILWAY WOOD SECTOR	21		Wind dangerous. Weather changeable. Patrol reconnoitred from ODER HOUSE & Kh MOUND & found no sign of the enemy. Unit relieved by 1K.L.R. & returned to YPRES.	
YPRES	22		Wind dangerous. Weather changeable, some snow. Cleaning up. Working parties. Ceremonial parade. Battalion addressed by the MAJOR GENERAL.	
	23		Wind dangerous. Weather fine. 1½ hours drill including Anti gas drill. Working parties. Coys at baths.	
	24		Wind dangerous. Weather changeable. 2¾ hours drill including Anti-gas drill. 1½ hours lecture. Working parties.	
	25		Wind dangerous. Weather changeable. Church Parade. Enemy shelled YPRES heavily.	
	26		Snow mostly continued, timepieces being changed at 11pm. & 12 midnight. Weather wet. A, B, C & D Coys. returned from 48 hours attachment to Heavy Artillery. 2½ hours drill including anti-gas drill. 3¼ hour lecture. Kings in the left sub-sector, right brigade sector, disposition of Companies being B, A, D, C, right front, left front, right support, & left support respectively. Night exceedingly quiet.	
RAILWAY WOOD SECTOR	27		Wind changeable. Weather fine. Some aeroplane activity, otherwise very quiet.	
	28		Wind slight. Weather changeable. Enemy trench & few A.A. and balloons up and aeroplanes in his rear quite	

Army Form C. 2118.

WAR DIARY
or
INTELLIGENCE SUMMARY.

(Erase heading not required.)

1/9th THE KINGS (LIV. Regt.) T.F.

March 1917

Place	Date	Hour	Summary of Events and Information	Remarks and references to Appendices
YPRES. RAILWAY WOOD SECTOR	29		Wind safer. Weather wet at first, changeable later. Slight enemy artillery & trench mortar & Machine Gun activity. Enemy sent up many flares at night. Enemy was noticed to expose himself at several places at STAND-TO. Own enemy Trench mortar activity.	Nil
	30		Wind safe. Weather variable, but generally fine & clear. Enemy patrol which approached our wire on left of Sub-sector A was dispersed by our Lewis Gun fire. Enemy shelled Battn HQrs at about 6pm. 2 O.Rs wounded.	Nil
	31st		Weather variable. Enemy artillery fairly active during the day & impacts directed at front line & communication trenches.	W.R.

F.M. Blair
Lieut Col.
Commanding 9th Kings

YM 24

15/5

CONFIDENTIAL.

War Diary
of
1/9 Liverpool R.
for the period
1st April to 30th April, 1917.

SECRET. 55th Division. No. 1525/2 (G).

G 7244

III Corps.

Under cover of a creeping barrage of 18 prs. with 4.5" Hows and Stokes Mortars firing upon selected points, a Fighting Patrol of 1 Officer and 7 Other Ranks of the 1/9th Liverpool Regiment entered the enemy's Sap at I.11.b.91.80. at 10.0 pm. last night.

The Sap was entered from the South side half way between its head and the enemy front line. Towards the Saphead two sentries were encountered who put up their hands when ordered and were taken prisoner. Towards the base of the Sap three more of the enemy were seen but they ran away when fired upon.

Having secured identification the patrol withdrew to our lines. The only casualty was one man of the covering party which consisted of 1 Officer and 10 Other Ranks, who was slightly wounded.

The wire where the patrol entered the sap was very bad and easy to surmount. The Sap itself is only about two feet deep with wooden floor boards.

Both prisoners belong to the 213th Regiment of the 207th Division which is normal. They give the order of battle from South to North as follows :-

209th Res. Inf. Regt. 213th Res. Inf. Regt. 65th Regt. This latter Regiment belongs to the 185th Division and would appear to confirm that the 17th Res. Division has been relieved in its Sector by the 185th Division.

All Officers, N.C.Os and Men who took part in this enterprise with the exception of two, were volunteers from 'C' Company which was the Company raided by the enemy on the 19th March.

55th Division. H.Q.
2nd April, 1917.

(Sd) J.K. COCHRANE, Col,
for Major General,
Commanding 55th Division.

Place	Date	Hour	Summary of Events and Information	Remarks and references to Appendices

Army Form C. 2118.

WAR DIARY or INTELLIGENCE SUMMARY
(Erase heading not required.)

9th Battn. The King's (Liverpool) Regiment

April 1917

Place	Date	Hour	Summary of Events and Information	Remarks
Railway Wood Sector YPRES	1/4/1917		Weather changeable. During the afternoon orders were issued for a fighting patrol to go out and endeavour to (1) Capture (2) Kill or capture its occupants, (3) to obtain identification from say at I.11.b.68.48. on S.W. edge No. 5 Crater. The patrol consisted of 1 Officer (2Lt. A.M. ADAMS) and of other ranks. At 9.58 p.m. our barrage commenced. At 10 p.m. patrol left our trenches and moved across NO MANS LAND toward and entered enemy defs at South side about midway between head and stoked prisoners. About 10 yards 2 sentries were encountered and only been away 13 minutes. The patrol then returned to our lines having operations. Our barrage was spasmodic throughout that put up by the enemy lit up very lights, breaking into two stars, were followed by a heavy barrage on our front line and CAMBRIDGE trench which lasted until 10.55 p.m. This was immediately carried out with only one man slightly wounded during the whole operations. A covering party was sent out thus south of No 5 Crater consisting of 1 officer (Lt. R.C.H. ELLAM, R.C.) and 10 other ranks to down the left flank of the fighting patrol. None of the enemy were encountered by the covering party. The Battalion was relieved on the Left Sub Sector at 2 a.m. on the night of the 1st/2nd. After relief it proceeded to billets at YPRES.	WR
YPRES	2nd to 6th		Large working parties were supplied by us during our tour in YPRES, work principally taking improvements of trenches, wiring etc. A certain amount of training (arms drill, box respirator drill, musketry etc) was also carried out daily although this was impeded somewhat by having to train under cover of billets etc. etc. The weather during this period was rather changeable with some snow. No casualties were sustained while the Battalion was in YPRES.	WR

Army Form C. 2118.

WAR DIARY
or
INTELLIGENCE SUMMARY

(Erase heading not required.)

1st Batt. The King's (Liverpool) Regiment

April 1917 (Ypres)

Instructions regarding War Diaries and Intelligence Summaries are contained in F.S. Regs., Part II. and the Staff Manual respectively. Title Pages will be prepared in manuscript.

Place	Date	Hour	Summary of Events and Information	Remarks and references to Appendices
YPRES	6th		During night of 6th/7th the Battalion was relieved by the 1/10 Bn. Liverpool (Scottish). Two companies "C" and "D" remained in YPRES and came under the command of CAPT. E. ASHTON. "B" Company entrained at YPRES at Q John and proceeded to PROVEN arriving there at 12 midnight. "A" Company and Battalion Headquarters entrained at YPRES detrained at BRANDHOEK and then marched to "C" Camp arriving about midnight.	R
"C" Camp	7th/14th		With the exception of an N.C.O.s class under the R.S.M. and Signalling class no training could be carried out owing to large working parties having to be found by the Battalion i.e. 230 other ranks work at YPRES, 100 other ranks working on new AERODROME at PROVEN and 160 other ranks working under R.E.s etc. on new Corps R.E. Park, Ammunition Dumps etc. Several lectures were arranged by officers and N.C.O.s class on Mining, Bayonet fighting etc. The following officers arrived as reinforcements: 8/4/17 – 2/Lt. H.T. DALLOW; 11/4/17 – 2/Lt. G.A. HENRY; 16/4/17 – 2/Lt. A.G. WARDE. The following officer was admitted to hospital on 14/4/17 – Lt. S.S. FAUSSET. On the 8th BRIG-GEN. F.J. DUNCAN. C.M.G. D.S.O proceeded to England and BRIG-GEN. L. BOYD-MOSS. CMG. assumed command of the 165th Infantry Brigade. The weather during above period was very changeable. "C" & "D" Companies at YPRES had no casualties although on several occasions they were heavily shelled and had to evacuate billets.	R R R R
"C" Camp	14th/18th		During the night of 14th/15th the Battalion moved up into Brigade Reserve at the ÉCOLE east of YPRES and took over billets from 1/5 King's Dispositions of our Companies being Battalion Headquarters, A, C & D Companies in the ÉCOLE, 2 platoons "B" Company in MENIN ROAD dugouts and 2 platoons in HALF MOON trench	R R

2449 Wt. W14957/M90 750,000 1/16 J.B.C. & A. Forms/C.2118/12.

Army Form C. 2118.

WAR DIARY
or
INTELLIGENCE SUMMARY

(Erase heading not required.)

Army Form C. 2118.

1/5th Batn. The King's (Liverpool) Regiment

3. April 1917

Place	Date	Hour	Summary of Events and Information	Remarks and references to Appendices
ECOLE, YPRES.	18th/23rd		During the tour in the ECOLE large working parties were supplied for carrying, improvement of trenches, wiring etc in Right Sub-Sector. A certain amount of training was carried out but owing to the area being under observation by the enemy the training had to be done under cover of billets etc. Church Parades, by Companies, were held in the ECOLE on the 22nd. The ECOLE was not shelled by enemy during occupation although a large number of 'blind' anti-aircraft shells fell in and around the ECOLE on the 22nd. The weather was fairly fine during the above period. No casualties were sustained.	10R.
	23rd		During the night battalion moved out of the ECOLE, the 1/4th King's taking over from us. We moved up into the Right Sub-Sector and relieved the 1/5th King's at Railway Wood the dispositions of our Companies being 'C' Company Right Front Company; 'D' Company Left Front Company; 'B' Company, Right Support Company; 'A' Company Left Support Company.	10 R.
RAILWAY WOOD SECTOR	24th/29		During the tour in RAILWAY WOOD numerous patrols were sent out, very good work being done. No enemy patrols were encountered. With the exception of two days enemy's light & heavy MINENWERFERS were extremely active, although the shooting was not very accurate. Considering the number of Mynen Werfers fired very little damage was done to our trenches. The enemy fired a considerable about 3 H.V. 36's. They also made strenuous endeavours to build dug-outs about 40 feet deep. As works were heard very low. Lt Carruthers was wounded 25th & 3 OR wounded. 26th 1 OR Killed & wounded. 29th 1 OR. Killed.	10 R.

2449 Wt. W14957/M90 750,000 1/16 J.B.C. & A. Forms/C.2118/12.

WAR DIARY or **INTELLIGENCE SUMMARY**

1/9th Battn. The King's (Liverpool) Regiment 1/9th Kings L'pool Regt T.F.

Army Form C. 2118.

APRIL (contd)

Place	Date	Hour	Summary of Events and Information	Remarks and references to Appendices
RAILWAY WOOD Sector	29th		During the night the Battalion was relieved by the 17th Bn THE KINGS L'pool Regt after which the Battn proceeded to YPRES and entrained at ASYLUM. Headquarters & A.B.C. entrained at BRANDHOEK & proceeded to "C" Camp arriving there at 3-30 A.M. D Coy proceeded by train direct to PROVEN arriving there at 2 A.M. During the relief the enemy put over a few MINENWERFERS and as the Coys were proceeding from the trenches to the ASYLUM the enemy commenced shelling the MENIN ROAD, ECOLE YPRES, with 4.2", 5.9", heavy artillery, fortunately the Coys arrived at RAILWAY without having any casualties.	W.K.
"C" Camp.	30th		Although the Battalion only arrived in Camp at 3-30 A.M., two working parties had to be supplied and it was necessary for one party to parade three hours afterwards to arrive at Rendezvous by time stated. 9 A.M. Remainder of Battalion was at disposal of Coy Cdrs. for Intended etc. Weather fine	W.K.

J.F. Dow
Lt Colonel
Cdg 1/9th King's L'pool Regt
T.F.

CONFIDENTIAL

War Diary
of
1/9th Liverpool R.
for the period
May 1st to 31st, 1917

WAR DIARY or INTELLIGENCE SUMMARY

Army Form C. 2118.

19th Batt. THE KINGS LPOOL REGT.

May 1917

Place	Date	Hour	Summary of Events and Information	Remarks and references to Appendices
6th Camp	1/5/17		During morning leaves granted to the three Companies in Camp. Proceeded to B Camp and saw our billets from the K.R.R. During the afternoon the three Companies were sent to the Baths.	N.R.
	2/5		Albert J. the Division had a very severe Marches out during the time it was in B Camp. excellent training was carried on in accordance with instructions laid down in "Offensive Action, Divl Genl, Bayd-Moor singled 19th Bn during the morning (of 1/5.) He remarked we were the smartest turned out he had ever seen. The Battalion has best of times 40 days, near Camagne, devoting from No training carried on in Tuesdays at our disposal.	N.R.
		9.40 a.m.	on the mrn of 5th to proceed an entraining at BRANDHOEK Station luck enemy & the enemy shells to line at YPRES, the train did not reach YPRES	
		10.40 a.m.	the Battalion detrained at Asylum, YPRES and proceeded to the trenches and relief of 1st 5th KING'S LPOOL REGT. Relief was completed	N.R.

Lee J. Am.

Army Form C. 2118.

WAR DIARY
or
INTELLIGENCE SUMMARY
(Erase heading not required.)

Instructions regarding War Diaries and Intelligence Summaries are contained in F.S. Regs., Part II. and the Staff Manual respectively. Title Pages will be prepared in manuscript.

Place	Date	Hour	Summary of Events and Information	Remarks and references to Appendices
	5.		During the relief the enemy shelled the MENIN ROAD area i.e. 11.42 every five minutes. However enemy shells were just the Pwouches were Lieutenants (D) Coy entering as BROKEN at 8.40.p.m. and joining the remains of Battalion at BRANDHOEK) The Battalion was organised into line being established in rear of POTIJZE. "D" Coy. in front line from I.J.D. 53. 30. to HAYMARKET extending "B" Coy. in support, "A" of JAMES TRENCH "C" and "D" Coys. in billets in YPRES.	N.F.
	6. to 11/5/17		During this tour in the line the weather was excellent. The enemy Artillery was not very active on our trenches but paid a great deal of attention to the town of YPRES, MENIN GATE and MENIN ROAD. A/11.c.m.on 7th for a practice Barrage was carried out on enemy trenches and orders were issued to Officers, N.C.O.'s and men of the Battalion to form an idea as to what a Barrage was like. At 8.45 P.M. and 11 P.M. our night out Artillery bombarded enemy's back area, their DUMPS & APPROACHES TO TRENCHES etc, with very good effect. Also the	N.F. N.F. N.F.

Army Form C. 2118.

WAR DIARY
or INTELLIGENCE SUMMARY
(Erase heading not required.)

1/9th Battn. THE KING'S (L'pool Regt.)

MAY, 1917.

Place	Date	Hour	Summary of Events and Information	Remarks and references to Appendices
RAILWAY WOOD SECTOR	6/5 4/5/17		Enemy shelled trenches & YPRES as he has done each night previously. Between 10.30 and 11.30 a.m. on the 4th enemy (about 70) gunners bombarded with 5.9 and 8" heavy gun trench fire (in & above) & shells a/bonk(?) fired. At 9.30 P.M. at night we blew a MINE in RAILWAY WOOD laying there was no artillery activity whatever. The following night a Camouflet was also blown by us. The two Companies in YPRES were ready also (or worked parties) and owing to the MINING they were Trenching with Carries out. A Cliff trench was Carried and they the two Companies on the line also a IMPRUDING pouring SHRAPNEL on Bombs, and MACHINE-GUNS. Casualties during this period were very light. 4th May one other rank DIED of wounds. One other rank wounded. 9th May one officer 2nd Lieut R.C.WHITE wounded (at Duty). Four other ranks wounded. 10th May 5 other ranks wounded. 12th and 1st Lieut R.Y.1, 13th & 24th wounded. During this last order was received to carry out a raid an enemy's trenches at OSKAR FARM. Pencil sketch were drawn in fear of a German bombardment & parties were detailed 3 Officers & 80 men (approx) by night. No MAN'S LAND was estimated 3 mths(?) Green to be 500 feet. Between 9 to 16 panels of 18 panels of wire cut and ...	R.O.

WAR DIARY
or
INTELLIGENCE SUMMARY.

(Erase heading not required.)

G.T. BATT. THE KING'S (L'POOL) REGT. T.F.

May 1917

Army Form C. 2118.

Place	Date	Hour	Summary of Events and Information	Remarks and references to Appendices
RAILWAY WOOD	10/5/17		excellent spirits. enemy's wire. At ZERO (11. PM) raiding party consisted of 2nd Lieut S.H. BANDIN, F.S. N. WADE and 40 other ranks left our trenches and proceeded across NO MAN'S LAND. Same time our Artillery put an excellent barrage on enemy trenches. Infantry perfectly supported this as planned. Enemy's wire found to be in good condition - only 3 men were found in the enemy's trenches - these were captured. Our trench barrage however caused casualties amongst 2nd Lieut WADE's party. Received in German trenches one died of his wounds. 2/Lt McADAM and another man with party held in reserve. Parties were sent for search. All telephone wires along trench also cut. 3rd Lieut WADE's party included 6 enlistees.	
dco 5.	11/5/17		One man was also a shelter for ammunition. Touched the enemy. They (three) eyed the enemy's trenches. Three were held. They immediately opened fire. They opened. So fiery immediately the enemy bombed the sleeping dug out finished. Shew in the trench. Entirely the small dump held and entered, and the enemy who opened fire on our advancing, a bombing division. C. Coy for wounded. A bomber easily detected were Cpl. F. NEVARD, Sgt. McCARTHY more against Pte. S. EDWARDS, L/Sgt. McCARTHY Pte. 38 Pte. new and 18 bombed the FOE 2 men dragged away. At 11.15 PM the force returned carrying all our men arrived back from their enterprise unharmed except for the wounded 2 been slightly wounded. OC the coy homes. Last 4 rifles 92.16.	

Army Form C. 2118.

WAR DIARY
or
INTELLIGENCE SUMMARY.

1/9th Batt. THE KING'S (L'Pool Regt.)

May 1917

(Erase heading not required.)

Place	Date	Hour	Summary of Events and Information	Remarks and references to Appendices
RAILWAY WOOD SECTOR "B" SECTOR	6/5/17 to 11/5/17		Found that the Prisoner captured the same morning, there were effectively dealt with. The enemy was a inferior division, evidently who accorded to prisoners statement. Surrendered Prisoners, and wounded were look to be 25% reported. There were at least 10 Prisoners Killed by M.G. bullets in this trench by his field howitzers the enemy have been Known as Oskar Farm Block & the Regiment mentioned as being by 2nd Lieut. A.T.D. From Duty are also officers that at the Rifle Equipment Box Regiment Col. Helmes Capt etc. They Cartridges belonged to the 1st Marine Infantry Regt. Communication was made with French Corps & Division & Brigade Commanders on the right. The Batt. were relieved by the Kings Own After 16 relief the Batt. proceeded to the ECOLE near Dickebusch. Ecole, etc, A Coy was in reserve on the Menin Rd and Hedge and J82-F Men Trenches During our way to the ECOLE Coys working parties were supplies A certain amount of training was also carried out.	Yes. Yes. Yes. Yes. Yes. Yes.
ECOLE	12/5/17 to 1/6			
	16/5/17		5th Bn. King's Own took the right 16/5/17 the Batt. were relieved by the Cambria Brigade in defensive in Lanes at the Asylum for Brandhoek arriving there at 2.30 a.m. The weather during the above days was very fine.	Yes.
B'Camp.	17/5/17		Poperinghe. The Batt. paraded at 9/15 and proceeded to H.T. Dns. They then marched for Wotten. Arriving there at The Transport proceed by road on the 16th. The Transport proceed by road on the 16th. Billets at BOLLEZEELE.	Yes.

2353 Wt. W25141/1454 700,000 5/15 D.D.&L. A.D.S.S./Forms/C. 2118.

Army Form C. 2118.

WAR DIARY
or
INTELLIGENCE SUMMARY.
(Erase heading not required.)

1/9th Batt. The King's (Liverpool Regt)

May 1917

Place	Date	Hour	Summary of Events and Information	Remarks and references to Appendices
BOLLEZEELE	17/5 to 31st		During our stay in BOLLEZEELE with the exception of one day, the weather was perfect with & we were therefore able to carry out a full day of training. The programme of one days work shewn is to Platoon training, Attack, Bayonet Fighting & Dummy Bomb, & Grenade Throwing & Specialist Training. Several drafts were also returned to Company. Strength of other ranks Rank & March was carried out Saturday the 26th inst. On the 27th the Battalion Sports were held in BOLLEZEELE & were a huge success. On the 22nd No Padre Service. Notified that the following N.C.O.'s & men had earned the Military Medal for Gallantry in Action as follows No.(tain) at OSKAR Farm near YPRES on the night of 11/11/16. 33767 Cpl. MCCARTHY S. 3306 Sh. Pte. FOULKES G. 3311 LA. MORRIS R. 3309 > S. SHIELDS F. Ten Gallantry Cards from Divisional Commander & six Letters of appreciation from Corps Commander were also received in connection with the above raid. The following Warrant Officer N.C.O's were sent home to England for General G.O.B Work:- Despatches for General G.O.B Work:- 330604 CSM & C.MENT J.M 330 Pte CPN & MEADONS J. 330 Pte Sgt. BALL T. C.SM. GRAYSON R.	initials initials

WAR DIARY
or
INTELLIGENCE SUMMARY

Army Form C. 2118.

Place	Date	Hour	Summary of Events and Information	Remarks and references to Appendices
BOLLEZEELE	17th to 3/8		On the 23rd inst. an O.R. Coy Wkly exercises in Light Toys men. by firing Rifle Grenades. On the 24th Wkl. Grenadiers were turned out by Brigade at MERCKEGHEM. On the 29th Brigade sports were upon Rifle Platoon win Drill etc. the whole of 5th Kings. Prize in R.W. I. Gun Competition in Rapid wire cutting & tying in Creations and Prize in Coy of Bat. Runners in Relay Race. Battn. was asked to see the official events. The Sergeants May a dinner and Entertainment stating the following Officers, N.C.O.s to be ccs. The MILITARY CROSS and D.C.M. respectively. 2nd Lieut. R. M. ADAMS } M.C. C. H. RANDALL } M.C. P. S. WARDE } SERGT. H. WILLIAMS D.C.M. has volunteered The above named were handed in Coy orders on the 1st and carried over by the units on the night of May 2nd May.	W.C. W. Pelier W.C. W.C.

J.M. Dew

Lieut. Col. Comdg.
19 Kings

CONFIDENTIAL

VA 26

War Diary
of
1/9th Liverpool R.
for the period
June 1st to June 30th. 1917

Army Form C. 2118.

WAR DIARY
or
INTELLIGENCE SUMMARY
(Erase heading not required.)

June 1917 HQ Bath. The Kings (Liverpool Regt.)

Place	Date	Hour	Summary of Events and Information	Remarks and references to Appendices
BOLLEZEELE	1st June to 11th		Our stay in BOLLEZEELE was much longer than earlier anticipated. 4 days in an area of training are carried out during the earlier period; and the Baths, laundries, &c. being ready by the 25 days of June from the scene. Training. The Bns work (Company in the attack), the Bns not certain, being done in Brigade in the afternoon, particular attention being paid to snipers. No Schools are regularly contained in parallel "Instructions for Platoon" as per Brigade. The training of the Lewis Section in its own weapon Bayonet fighting, Revolver, be bring for numbers 1 and 3 of the Lewis Gun team, Close Order Drill, Van and Rear of Arms and saluting into Section during the afternoon each Section was allowed to carry out its own programme of training under a resident officer. The Brigade Ripicti Runners Coy held very good training in NO MEAN's MORE and NO MAN's Readers Landing etc. On Saturdays June 9th 3 Companies went for a 10 mile Route March. The following Reinforcement Camp for this month: Div. Reinforcements Reinforcements arrived after	
			2 O.R.	
			6 O.R.	
			100 O.R.	
			1 O.R.	
			19 O.R.	

WAR DIARY or INTELLIGENCE SUMMARY

Army Form C. 2118.

(Erase heading not required.)

1/6 Green Howards (Yorks Regt)

June 1917

Place	Date	Hour	Summary of Events and Information	Remarks and references to Appendices
BOLLEZEELE	June 6 1917		During the morning orders were received from Bgde that the Transport would move independently to HERZEELE in the afternoon. The following day the remainder of Bn would move from HERZEELE to Transport lines at G.5.c. east of POPERINGHE. The Bn. paraded at 8 a.m. & marched to HERZEELE Y entraining up to a.m. for POPERINGHE, arriving & .... at 1.30 P.M. They marched to B. Camp where the training men lived. They remained at B. Camp until 11.30 P.M. They proceeded to BRANDHOEK STN. to entrain for YPRES, but owing to a break-down on the line at POPERINGHE Ry .... were due to entrain until 1.15 am. Arrived & ..... Railway Crossing between HOMERTINGHE & YPRES, the Bn. (....... march) to the trenches relieving the 11/K.L.W. KMCR in the POTIJZE Sector. Owing to that .... being neither complete enough to draw the Trenches in ..... of 1/K.L.W. KMCR were asked to remain in paint of the .... to relig told me .... a full amount of Relieving of each area performed by the Battn. was very satisfactory throughout and following to commence the YPRES area of the ..... when 2 Coy on the right	

WAR DIARY or INTELLIGENCE SUMMARY

Army Form C. 2118.

19th Bn. The King's (Liverpool Regt.)

June 1917

Place	Date	Hour	Summary of Events and Information	Remarks and references to Appendices
	11/6 1/6/17		From PICCADILLY TRENCH to (2) HAYMARKET TRENCH. C Coy Left from HAYMARKET to NORWICH FARM. B Coy in support in ST JAMES TRENCH. and Q Coy in reserve at of the POTIJZE Road. Battn Headquarters at POTIJZE (I 30.5.8). Relief complete on 2nd 6th when Lt. Col. Whent proceeded on leave to England. Major Worrell assumed command of the Battn.	
POTIJZE Sector	11/6 to 15/6/17		During this tour in the trenches the 17th TUNNELLING Coy R.E. have been very active indeed on their various approaches underneath BEAR ALLAO YPRES BATH. Road etc. A German aeroplane being brought down on the 13th at 3 am and also has been very active on the 15th as (17th) as 3.10am and 3.10am respectively. Several MINES were blown by the Germans opposite the RAILWAY Sector. Early in the morning of the 13th between 2 and 3 am. the Bosch blew 5 MINES which appears to be between his front line and support line opposite the Scots actually in reports 2 to each battery tally. Although enemy artillery has been to action specially to concentrate has been sustained by the enemy Vizi- 1.O.R.	
WIELTJE Sector	15/6/17 15/6/17		Scots by the 1/5th KING'S OWN. Relief complete with those During the night 14/6/17 (Sid Battn being relieved in the THIRD line by the 5th Bn SHERWOOD FORESTERS or by 10 pm. and refers to the 7th Bn SHERWOOD FORESTERS proceeded to WIELTJE Sector and relieved LH by the 5th KING'S OWN. Relief completed at 2am. and on relief the 1/7th Sherwood Foresters by 3.10am	

Army Form C. 2118.

WAR DIARY
or
INTELLIGENCE SUMMARY.
(Erase heading not required.)

Instructions regarding War Diaries and Intelligence Summaries are contained in F. S. Regs. Part II. and the Staff Manual respectively. Title pages will be prepared in manuscript.

June 1917.

Place	Date	Hour	Summary of Events and Information	Remarks and references to Appendices
WIELTJE Sect.	1/9/17		The dispositions of our Companies being:- "B" Coy on the Right from NEW JOHN ST. to the ST. JULIEN ROAD, "A" Coy on the left front from the ST. JULIEN ROAD to C.22.D.0.5.27. "C" Coy in support in LIVERPOOL TRENCH with one Platoon on Nore Farm in the ST. JEAN Defences, and "D" Coy in reserve at ST. JEAN opposite POTIJZE ROAD at I.3.D.30.30. Regt. H.Q. remained at POTIJZE (16.5.½) Batt'n Headquarters of this sector have are 2 posts, one in support of the Ypres line, made up the Officers of "B" Coy now being down. The difference position (of the various D.O's Rifle Grenades were fired by the enemy, at one of these posts, Lewis [?] came through into Dublin). Owned the Town in this sector — the whole of its Artillery has been increased. Enemy aircraft very active. The H.Q. of the 17th Can. Men here-of LOCOMOTORY SHEEL (No. 3 Battalion) PUTNZ E N.Q.A. II.C.[?] Therefore necessary for Bon. [?] to be brought approximately 130 men are carried daily, for supplies in the Lines [?]. The supplies and 3rd [?] battalion for sappers come the [?] where have they been men were neere [?] yet was on the Trenches	Keeper [?] Post P.R. P.R. B.C. B.C. [signatures]

2353 Wt. W.2517/1454 700,000 5/15 D. D. & L. A.D.S.S./Forms/C. 2118.

Army Form C. 2118.

WAR DIARY
or
INTELLIGENCE SUMMARY.
(Erase heading not required.)

[...] "A" Sqn. The King's [...]

Place	Date	Hour	Summary of Events and Information	Remarks and references to Appendices
MELNIE (cont'd)	16/6/17		Orders were received from Brigade that HOPKIN TRENCH was now to be occupied #1 (1st Troop) in front of the 2/5th Glosters (Sqn) had to be increased. All available men (about 25) were to defend (a) top of this report and an average of about 50 pivots 1 × 3ft × 2ft were dug each night. PATROLS were sent out nightly through & round the Bosch wire in this sector. The following Casualties were sustained:—	R.R. W.O. R.R. W.O.
			2nd LIEUT. A.F. MORTON) 2nd " M.P. DALLOW) and 5. O.R. wounded) 1. C.S.M. and 1. Sergeant 2nd " R.C.H. EALAM) 1. O.R. AT DUTY. 1. O.R. Died of Wounds. 3. O.R. Evacuated	R.R. W.O.
	17/6/17 18/6/17		What artillery activity occurred in the Line rather longer than usual. The General Feeling in the Sqn. was that the 20th Bav. Div. Res. had been relieved about the 20th last in the line. There was no opportunity of getting in touch with the enemy so as to obtain identifications to this effect.	R.R. W.O.
	19/6/17 20/6/17		Fairly heavy Artillery fire & a few Generally rounds of damaged our line to our trenches. On the 25th no less than 200 Shells including 60. 8 inch. & several hundred 5.9 fire	R.R. W.O.

Army Form C. 2118.

WAR DIARY
or
INTELLIGENCE SUMMARY.
(Erase heading not required.)

June 1917. /Capt. [signature]

Instructions regarding War Diaries and Intelligence Summaries are contained in F.S. Regs., Part II. and the Staff Manual respectively. Title pages will be prepared in manuscript.

Place	Date	Hour	Summary of Events and Information	Remarks and references to Appendices
NIEILTJE Sector.	18/6/17 to 30/6/17		On the trench system, NIEILTJE Sr. at POTIJZE was also thoroughly shelled almost every night and also during the day. A number of GRANATENWERFERS were fired almost every night on roving party out in front of our front line. On the night of 24/5/17 2/Lt Jenkins Lewis Gunners & 2nd Lieuts DEY and MORSON and 20 O.Rs. made proceeded to C.29.a.05.96. to C.29.a.10.90. with the intention of making enemy working party. Where wounded they proceeded to the trenches on the known worth path where Wounded got out. They had been driven in evidently found Otherwise. They soon saw that they had been driven in evidently Jelly Well did & sent some parties out. On Patrol Extremely Complete. A large enemy party was careful but the Parties did during the own troops. Bt. men 8 & the 165. M.G.C. Ret men were attacked. The. 19, Trench Bu "Cay". (Trench 159 men to work left the NIEILTJE ESTAMINET supplied. Referring to machine gun fire in proximity at Key Track was add in the front of the front line numbered from C.2.F.2.50.10. via ARGYLE FARM & west of LYTHAM CR. Range C.2. & 30.30. The work trench and a step to give effect of cover. The direction of Trench of about 200 yards the trench was completed by the end of the month. The NIEILTJE object was made to Lou. Bay; all the arrangement even taken down and Rifle fitted. The machine during this period was very changeable.	[initials] W.R. [initials] W.R. [initials] W.R. [initials] W.R. [initials] W.R. [initials] W.R.

Army Form C. 2118.

WAR DIARY
or
INTELLIGENCE SUMMARY.
(Erase heading not required.)

1/9th Bn. The King's (Liverpool) Regt.

Place	Date	Hour	Summary of Events and Information	Remarks and references to Appendices
NIEUPORT	June 1917			
	30/6/17		The following Casualties were sustained:—	
			(9th) 2 O.R. Killed and 2 O.R. wounded. (S.I.W.)	
			(10th) 1 O.R. Killed, and 4 O.R. wounded. (1 acc. Duty)	
			(17th) 2 O.R. wounded.	
			(22nd) 2/Lieut. N.M. GREEVES wounded, 1 O.R. (killed) and 3 O.R. wounded	
			(23rd) 2 O.R. wounded. (1 at Duty)	
			(25th) 4 O.R. wounded. (2 at Duty)	
			(26th) 6 O.R. wounded. (1 at Duty)	
			(27th) 3 O.R. wounded. (1 at Duty)	
			(29th) 2 O.R. wounded.	
			(30th) 5 O.R. wounded.	
			(30th) Capt E. ASHTON wounded.	
			Casualties of the Transport Section during the month have been very light	
			considering the amount of shelling the Section has been subjected to	
			here. During this period the Transport has had (1 O. killed, 1 Driver	
			and 1 Mule killed) They had a hit on the right of 29/30, having	
			1 killed & 3 Transport Coys — ordinary trench work did not come under	
			any undue shelling during the period.	
			On the night 29/30. An enemy patrol were sent out eighty	
			strong. Our patrol advanced close to our listening post	

2353 Wt. W2544/1454 700,000 5/15 D.D.&L. A.D.S.S./Forms/C. 2118.

Army Form C. 2118.

WAR DIARY
or
INTELLIGENCE SUMMARY
(Erase heading not required.)

Instructions regarding War Diaries and Intelligence Summaries are contained in F. S. Regs., Part II. and the Staff Manual respectively. Title Pages will be prepared in manuscript.

June 1917.   1/5th Bn. The King's (Liverpool Regt.)

Place	Date	Hour	Summary of Events and Information	Remarks and references to Appendices
NIEULLE St. Vaast			At LYNGEM C.T. Patrol was fired at, and dispersed by one of our Lewis Guns. The Patrol of enemy immediately came at to find Out if any of the enemy had been wounded; with the exception of a few Cap. & German Rifles, (gun & clean), was no identification. The Head cools be found. The following Reinforcements arrived as Reinf. Reg. Camp for the week:	
	3/6/17		4 O.R.	
	7/6/17		1 O.R.	
	27/6/17		5 O.R.	
	30/6/17		20 O.R. (These men & grades to Transport Section)	
	28/6/17		Lieut. Col. Bates returned from leave and resumed command of the Battn.	
	15/30/17		Inter-Company Reliefs were carried out every few days	
	25/6/17		2/Lts C B JOHNSON & J EBBELS were transferred from the BORDER REGT to this Unit. Capt. E G HOARE was-o appointed acting Major and second in command from 15.4.17	

J.K. Dean
Lieut Colonel
Commanding 1/5 Bn The King's (L'pool Regt.) T.F.

In the Field
1.7.19.17

Vol 27.

War Diary
of the
1/9 Liverpool R.
for the period
1st July to 31st July
1917.

Army Form C. 2118.

WAR DIARY
or
INTELLIGENCE SUMMARY.

(Erase heading not required.)

1/9th The West Kent Regt.

July 1917.

Instructions regarding War Diaries and Intelligence Summaries are contained in F. S. Regs., Part II. and the Staff Manual respectively. Title pages will be prepared in manuscript.

Place	Date	Hour	Summary of Events and Information	Remarks and references to Appendices
WELTJE	1/9/1917 12.30		Enemy artillery was fairly active during this period, and on the night 2nd/3rd the Batt. was relieved by the 2/5th Lou: Fusiliers, relief complete at 3 am. During the night of relief enemy available men were working on the line. Between the trench was completed before the Batt. left the line. Owing to it being daylight by the time the Batt. was relieved it was necessary for men to proceed in small parties and as the roads were being shelled by the enemy, the Overland Tracks were used. The Batt. was reported present in "Query" Camp at 6 am on the morning of the 3rd. At the Batt. had to be clear of Query Camp by 12 noon we moved to field in the vicinity of the camp. The mounted men and cookers having at 3.30 pm. The Battn. proceeded to BRANDHOEK STATION and entraining here at 7.30 pm. The men by route march to BOISDIGHEM	SHEET 28.N.W. BELGIUM.
Query Camp.			drawn, the officers marched to the vicinity of the camp. The mounted men and cookers left at 3.30 pm. The Battn. proceeded to BRANDHOEK STATION and entraining here at 7.30 pm. The men by route march to LUMBRES, arriving HAZEBROUCK arriving at 7.30 pm. Thence by route march to BOISDIGHEM arriving at the latter place at 10.45 pm. The Bn. were watching	SHEET 20. N.W. BELGIUM. 5A

Army Form C. 2118.

WAR DIARY
or
INTELLIGENCE SUMMARY.
(Erase heading not required.)

July 1917 ....

Place	Date	Hour	Summary of Events and Information	Remarks and references to Appendices
BOISDINGHEM			and were ready for a rest after having done 22 days in the front line system, during which time they had been subjected to rather heavy shelling & also they had had very little sleep for 2 days.	HAZEBROUCK 5a
BOISDINGHEM	3rd 5th 6th		During our stay in this Village, a Church hut & workshops & Companies were at disposal of Company Commanders for cleaning up, organizing, reequipping etc. The billets in the village were quite good, the weather was very fine.	
MORINGHEM	6th		At 11.30 am the Battn. paraded and marched to Moringhem. There was ample accommodation in this village for HQ & three Companys in billets. One Company bivouaced, & Company accommodated in tents.	MORINGHEM HAZEBROUCK 5a
"	7th 8th 9th 10th		During our stay in this village practise in the attack was carried out under Brigade arrangements, each Batln. operating on the front that was to be allotted to it in the attack.	

WAR DIARY
or
INTELLIGENCE SUMMARY.

(Erase heading not required.) 11gA The King's (Lpool Regt.)

Army Form C. 2118.

July 1917

Place	Date	Hour	Summary of Events and Information	Remarks and references to Appendices
MORINGHEM	7th		A Special Training Area was allotted to the Brigade for the Rehearsal of the Attack. This area being nearly clearly on the Topo. Notes. Boards indicating the objectives that the Brigade would be allotted during the actual Attack were erected, and practices every man in the Battalion fully acquainted with the area and with other troops engaged & them during the actual show. The scheme was very keen and in every way proved to be of a huge success. The weather during the period was generally warm with occasional showers of rain. Unfortunately a lift was not available for taking men on hot occasions. Sundays 15 & 22 & 76th Company Marches in depently & Moule for bathing On the 5th a representative of & Queen C. & being drawn.	HAZEBROUCK 5.9

Army Form C. 2118.

WAR DIARY
or
INTELLIGENCE SUMMARY.
(Erase heading not required.)

G.H.Q Mules & Goods Dist. July 1917

Place	Date	Hour	Summary of Events and Information	Remarks and references to Appendices
MORINGHEM	19th		On the 9th & 10th 2 token Disinfections was allowed to this unit, every mans clothing was put through the Foden process, & all riminous clothing was effectually dealt with. The Leave allotment during this period was exceptionally good.	HAZEBROUCK 59 10/G 10/G
D°	21st		The Bath. paraded at 8 am and marched to ST-OMER entraining there at 11 am arriving at POPERINGHE about 3 pm. thence by route march to "B" Camp. 2½ K. the exception of Cookers Water Cart, Medical Cart Mess Cart & 5 Wagons which proceeded by rail. the Transport proceeded by road from MORINGHEM on the 19th inst.	ST OMER 16S/F
"B" Camp.	28th		During our Stay in "B" Camp training was carried out under Company arrangements, particular attention being paid to the Lewis Gunners. On the 23rd inst 1 n.c.o. & 1 everything party of 50. O.Ranks was supplied for work with the R.E.s	SHEET 28. N.W BELGIUM. 16S/F

WAR DIARY or INTELLIGENCE SUMMARY

Army Form C. 2118.

(Erase heading not required.)

19th Batt. "The Lens" Local Regt.

Place	Date	Hour	Summary of Events and Information	Remarks and references to Appendices
'B' Camp	July 1917		at POTIJZE DUMP.	SHEET 28. N.W. Cone & Sheet BELGIUM
			On the 24th One Company was sent up to the Baths Coy. for work. This Coy. reforms to Baker Con. 29th On the 19th A working party of 200. O. Ranks was sent to POTIJZE for Cable-burying. The party was sent back to Camp at 11 P.M. arriving at 3.30 a.m on the 28th On the night of 27th Aeroplanes (enemy) dropped bombs in the vicinity of the Camp at least five in the Camp & wounded 2 Officers and 2 Other Ranks. The following reinforcements joined the Battn during the month:-	
			4th ... 109 O. Ranks	23rd 1 Reinforcement arrived at Dunesbach Reinf & Convent Camp for duty with the Battn during the month.
			7th ... 22 "	
			9th ... 29 "	
			14th ... 2 "	
			17th ... 14 "	

Army Form C. 2118.

WAR DIARY
or
INTELLIGENCE SUMMARY.
(Erase heading not required.)

July 1917

Place	Date	Hour	Summary of Events and Information	Remarks and references to Appendices
"B" Camp	20th to 28th		The following Casualties were sustained during the month:-	SHEET 28. N.W. BELGIUM
			2nd Lieut :- 1 OR Wounded	
			9th do 1 OR Wounded	
			9th do 1 OR Wounded	
			5 OR Wounded (Killed during operations & work	
			west of Tunnelling Co Royal Engineers during the month)	
	27.		Capt. S.J. Ferry. Wounded	
			Lieut. S.F. Forrest. do (at duty) By Enemy	
			1 O.R. Died of Wounds. Aeroplane	
			1. " Wounded. Bomb	
D°	29th		The Batt:n moved from "B"Camp to Derham Redoubt. H.Q.C.Y.D. (also the party to be Lift Bn. of Cotrs.) arriving here at 10.30pm. The party to be Wp.f. O.A. of Ashton proceeded to the Transport men at EDWARDHOEK.	
Durham D. Redoubt	30th		During the day the Transport lines moved from EDWARDHOEK to VLAMERTINGHE. At 6.30pm the Batt:n proceeded	

Army Form C. 2118.

WAR DIARY
or
INTELLIGENCE SUMMARY.
(Erase heading not required.)

8/7 The King's (L'pool Regt)

July 1917.

Place	Date	Hour	Summary of Events and Information	Remarks and references to Appendices
Durham Redoubt	30th		by Platoons to OXFORD TRENCH. Took up their positions ready for the attack the following morning.	Tues 28! N.H. BELGIUM N.H.
OXFORD TRENCH	31st		The Battalion in action. No details to hand.	

J.H. Dun

John Rees
Aug 1st 1917

Lieut Colonel Commanding
8/7 The King's L'pool Regt
J.R.

War Diary
of
1/9th Liverpool R.
for period
1st to 31st August, 1917.

Army Form C. 2118.

WAR DIARY
or
INTELLIGENCE SUMMARY.
(Erase heading not required.)

1/9 the Kings (pool Reg)

August 1917

Place	Date	Hour	Summary of Events and Information	Remarks and references to Appendices
OXFORD TRENCH	July 31		The Battalion went into action as follows:—	
			Headquarters. Major E.G. HOARE in Command	
			Capt. F. ATKINSON 2nd in Command	
			2nd Lieut C.B. JOHNSON Adjutant	
			2nd Lieut N. LEES Lewis Gun Officer	
			Lieut. G.W. HARRISON Medical Officer	
			A Company	
			2nd Lieut W.L. GELDARD in Command	
			2nd " S.M. RANDALL	
			" " J.H. RAVCLIFFE	
			" " G.A. HENRY	
			B Company 2nd Lieut E. TOWLE in Command	
			" " R.H. ELAM	
			2nd " J.K. EBBELS	
			" " T.H. LLOYD	

WARDIARY
or
INTELLIGENCE SUMMARY

Army Form C. 2148.

August 1917

Place	Date	Hour	Summary of Events and Information	Remarks and references to Appendices
	July 31st		C Company	
			Captain L.L.S. ARCHER	
			2nd Lieut W.L. BARKER	
			2nd " T.E. HICKSON	
			2nd " H.E. DAY	
			D Company	
			Captain E.H.G ROBERTS	
			Lieut. S.S. TAUSSAT	
			2nd Lieut F.J. MAURICE	
			2nd " R.C. WHITE	

Army Form C. 2118.

WAR DIARY
or
INTELLIGENCE SUMMARY. /9th "The Kings" Liverpool Regt.
(Erase heading not required.)

August 1917.

Instructions regarding War Diaries and Intelligence Summaries are contained in F. S. Regs., Part II. and the Staff Manual respectively. Title pages will be prepared in manuscript.

Place	Date	Hour	Summary of Events and Information	Remarks and references to Appendices
	JULY 31st 1917		Personnel awards 1/R.S.M. Roberts D. Sgt Faber G.F.	
OXFORD TRENCH.	JULY 30 1917		The Battalion proceeded into the BLACK LINE from D.24.d.35.55. to D.19.a.40.45. The moving up was from OXFORD TRENCH, Battalion Headquarters being in the East dugout. All dispositions were completed by about 2.30 AM. – The first wave was composed of C. Company on the left (LEFT) and D. Company on the right (RIGHT) with a platoon from B. Company under 2nd Lieut Erskine in rear to mop up PLUM FARM and APPLEVILLA. B. Company was in support and A. Company in reserve. At 3.0 AM ten wire ironed, and the leaving wave got out of OXFORD TRENCH and lay in front of 15R	

Army Form C. 2118.

WAR DIARY
or
INTELLIGENCE SUMMARY.
(Erase heading not required.)

Instructions regarding War Diaries and Intelligence Summaries are contained in F. S. Regs., Part II. and the Staff Manual respectively. Title pages will be prepared in manuscript.

Army 1917   10th The Kings Regt

Place	Date	Hour	Summary of Events and Information	Remarks and references to Appendices
	JULY 1917 30		Zero hour was fixed for 3.50 A.M. when the 5th and 6th Kings would have to attack and capture the German front line system and consolidate the BLUE LINE. The night was quiet, and the Battalion had got into position without casualties. At 3.50 A.M. the barrage started	
	July 31st 1917		and the 5th & 6th Kings left the Trenches. Our Artillery was to lift OXFORD TRENCH to take up their position in WARWICK TRENCH. At 4.20 A.M. the Battalion started. It was very dark and difficult to pick up landmarks. No news had yet come in from the 5th & 6th Kings. Four minutes after ZERO, the enemy put a heavy barrage of H.E. Shell on OXFORD TRENCH — Several men were hit here, a Lewis Gun Team was knocked out, and the reserve Lewis gun ammunition blown up. The air was in PAGODA STREET had previously been blown up, and the prisoners had to be placed in the open trench. No news came in for a	

WAR DIARY or INTELLIGENCE SUMMARY

Army Form C. 2118.

(Erase heading not required.)

for the King's Own Regt.
August 1917.

Place	Date	Hour	Summary of Events and Information	Remarks and references to Appendices
	JULY 31 1917		Long time, but numbers of Germans prisoners have been coming over to our lines.	
		AM 6-30	At 6.30 A.M. Capt. Atkinson, Lieut P.V. Johnson, 2nd Lt. Lees, and 2/Lieut. Roberts went over to establish Brigade Headquarters at JASPER FARM. No news was received from these 6th or 9th until 7.30 A.M. when a runner returned	
		AM 7.30	from Capt. Atkinson bringing message from the front line that "B" Coy. Atkinson reported that "C" Coy. Pickett reported that to Companies and supports had reached his objective but was in need of reinforcements. Capt. ROBERTS reported that he had crossed the STEENBEKE with from 6 to 10 men. Another message following immediately on that to that reached BANK FARM. 2nd Lieut. GELDERD reported that he had reached his final objective with 7(?) men. Headquarters then proceeded then to JASPER FARM, and then to a dugout near JASPER FARM. A message was then received that 2nd Lieut ELLAM had reinforced 2nd Lt UHLAN	

Army Form C. 2118.

WAR DIARY
or
INTELLIGENCE SUMMARY.
(Erase heading not required.)

Instructions regarding War Diaries and Intelligence Summaries are contained in F. S. Regs., Part II. and the Staff Manual respectively. Title pages will be prepared in manuscript.

Place	Date	Hour	Summary of Events and Information	Remarks and references to Appendices
	July 31st 1917		2nd Lieut GEUDER with fifty (50) men and that all were consolidated. A runner reported that D. Company had been held up by a machine gun in both flanks, but the men who had been temporarily held up were reforming their company in small parts. At this time the enemy was shelling his old front line system NO MAN's LAND and our back as POTIJZE very heavily with 77mm, 4.2, 5.9 and 8 inch shell in addition to high-bursting shrapnel. In the vicinity of JASPER FARM there were five (5) tanks, most of which appeared to be derelicts.	
		9.30 am	A message was received at 9.30 am from 2nd Lt. EBBELS who with his platoon was at APPLE VILLA, saying that the enemy was massing on HILL 35 - at the same time the 10th BRIGADE was seen to attack the GREEN LINE began to pass JASPER FARM. A verbal message was received saying that	R.K.

WAR DIARY
or
INTELLIGENCE SUMMARY.
(Erase heading not required.)

Army Form C. 2118.

"9th" The Kings Liverpool Regt

Place	Date	Hour	Summary of Events and Information	Remarks and references to Appendices
	July 31st 1917		Lieut FAUSSET had been killed and 2/Lt BARKER wounded. 2nd Lieut RAWCLIFFE was slightly wounded.	
		AM 11.45	At 11.45 AM, orders arrived from the Brigade that all available men were to be sent up to the BLACK LINE and that we were to be reinforced by two (2) Companies of the 62 Kings. Major HOARE then went forward by PLUM FARM to BANK FARM and the POMMERN REDOUBT to see what the situation was — at PLUM FARM there were orders wounded and Lieut HARRISON established an Aid Post there in a concrete dugout. BANK FARM had been captured by this Battalion although it was really in the sector allotted to the 166 Brigade. A German machine gunner on the roof of a concrete dugout had caused us many casualties — in carrying out the attack on this gun Lieut FAUSSET who led the party was shot through the ear — a Tank arrived at the	

WAR DIARY or INTELLIGENCE SUMMARY

Army Form C. 2118.

"A" Coy 1/9th Cheshire Regt Capt ...
August 1917

Place	Date	Hour	Summary of Events and Information	Remarks and references to Appendices
	July 31 1917		noticed movement and that the machine gunner who had been firing his gun salvo to the last minute and was lying dead by the roof of the dugout surrounded by hundreds of empty cases. Capt. ROBERTS has also come up against BANK FARM, whereupon 2nd Lieut GELDERD seeing that the leading companies were going too far to the left (LEFT) attacked the POMMERN REDOUBT with six men one of them being a signaller armed with a Shutta. Wounded they captured about forty prisoners. Then 2nd Lieut Elliot arrived with B Company and the number of prisoners was increased to about 90 (ninety). The enemy was quite demoralized and running in crowds over the crest line of Hill 35. 2nd Lieut RANDALL had led an attack on a party of Germans who started bombing our men on their left flank as they were digging in. BANK FARM. Capt ROBERTS saw a party of Germans lying in a trench. He immediately rushed forward them shouting	

WAR DIARY
or
INTELLIGENCE SUMMARY.
(Erase heading not required.)

Army Form C. 2118.

Instructions regarding War Diaries and Intelligence Summaries are contained in F. S. Regs., Part II. and the Staff Manual respectively. Title pages will be prepared in manuscript.

Place	Date	Hour	Summary of Events and Information	Remarks and references to Appendices
	July 31, 1917.		No. 1 Section who were now quite isolated "froze tooth, nail" – the Germans at once took up a close setting up their Lewis Guns & "Koch Loch Loch" and surrendered. During the attack on the POMMERN REDOUBT Corporal JAMES CLARK obtained an enemy machine gun team being to fire their gun out of action – he immediately shot one of the enemy and the remainder took flight and carried them to surrender their guns. At the same place Serjt. Jas Brunel MACREYBANK organised a bombing squad and worked his way down an enemy trench – this squad although under severe fire, took twenty (20) prisoners. Three (3) former GOD displayed great gallantry in leading the enemy and blasting the supply of bombs was finished he went German bombs throwing his efforts at least a dozen prisoners were taken. The Companies were reorganised and were ordered to occupy the line from BANK FARM to the POMMERN REDOUBT – This was	

Army Form C. 2118.

WAR DIARY
or
INTELLIGENCE SUMMARY.
(Erase heading not required.)

Instructions regarding War Diaries and Intelligence Summaries are contained in F. S. Regs., Part II. and the Staff Manual respectively. Title pages will be prepared in manuscript.

Army Corps _____
Division _____
August 1917

Place	Date	Hour	Summary of Events and Information	Remarks and references to Appendices
	JUNE 31st 1917	11. A.M.	Anthony Leach-Whelan from 11 A.M. till 4 P.M. Company did war instruction in a dugout at BANK FARM on the way of showing me the machine gun which had caused so much trouble. This August had been the Leach Gunnery of our artillery officers believed to be a Colonel who was taken prisoner by Sergeant Williams. A number of many enemy aeroplanes were later here and sent down by the Brigade.	
		4 P.M.	Now station at PLUM FARM. Clearer & rain reports began to come in that things were not going well outside the 167th Brigade in front of us and that we were falling back and for some time no confirmation of this with information. Cavalry Commanders were warned to be ready in case of counter attack - it was the time the situation on our front was impossible to see anything clearly some patrols were out on the left parties of Germans could be seen some	

WAR DIARY
or
INTELLIGENCE SUMMARY

Army Form C. 2118.

Place	Date	Hour	Summary of Events and Information	Remarks and references to Appendices
	JULY 31 1917		It was evidently contemplated that the enemy would had been driven to the high ground about REZENBERG & there reinforced to be to his front. The advance to the Brigade was to be on the line being taken from Hill 38 Jun. The was not now to be from Cheverial. Jetley Cemetery was therefore to met at one cost with the nineteenth during the advance and with the machine Brigade was pushed in to the army here having Hill 37 in front. On October sixth arrived from the Bridge taken no general advance up to the BLAIR LINE having enemy that was effected in many the BROODSEINDE away to shell it. It was ordered by further ORDER sweeping up to the Brigade was to be delivered that night	
	EVENING			

Army Form C. 2118.

WAR DIARY
or
INTELLIGENCE SUMMARY.
(Erase heading not required.)

August 1917

Place	Date	Hour	Summary of Events and Information	Remarks and references to Appendices
	JULY 31		Heavy shelling to prevent the arrival of reinforcements.	
			BATTN. H.Q. who slowed down such and the for the	
			Meeting and now very much all round TURN FARM as	
			Early of 20 (Thirty) horse there sent to from the forward	
			camp/a at 6.C. — in view their they are Enough all but 3	
			(there) were casualties might (3) at there hens twenty	
	NIGHT.		During the night the 164 Brigade relied over the BLACK	
			LINE and rain fell heavily.	
	AUGUST 1		At daybreak Orders for the advance of min. Second became known and two	
			(2) Derelict TANKS in the quest of Hill 35. but it was	
			uncertain where these were moving at men belonging to the	
			164 Brigade were still heavily through their success	
			from the rain. Owing to their very bad condition already as the VALLEY of	
			the STENBEKE — the Troops were fully and exhausted the	
			were beginning to crumble in the mud had been rescued	
			and no shelter had they home talking in the water	

Army Form C. 2118.

WAR DIARY
or
INTELLIGENCE SUMMARY.
(Erase heading not required.)

August 1917   John A. Lee for B. Coy 14th

Instructions regarding War Diaries and Intelligence Summaries are contained in F. S. Regs., Part II. and the Staff Manual respectively. Title pages will be prepared in manuscript.

Place	Date	Hour	Summary of Events and Information	Remarks and references to Appendices
	AUG 1st 1917		Shortly daylight enemy shelling heavily shelled	
		AFTERNOON	by the enemy most uncomfortable in consequence	
			Twin Crater reorganised rations and fresh food in comfortable	
			NO MANS LAND but S.O. and Sergeant Gittles on platform	
			lost large pail & half of mostly common here deserved	
		EVENING	My TEAM PARTY shelling up very slightly fortunately no	
			killed tonight advance party sent over 70 legs enemy	
			the day AUG (2) Sergeant GRIFFITHS and fellow E.S. took over	
			Twin Crater about two hours no casualty inflicted	
			took such a rest B. pushing forward but strong front	
		NIGHT AUG 1st/2nd		the rest of HILL 35 by the night of the 1st/2nd in depth	
			but our women and some E.S.B.'s but continued to stay	
			the everywhere holding HILL 35	
	AUG 2nd	About 5.AM. A savage counter from the Bruges from	
			that the various of the carrow woods two enemy inf	
			where the Lewis touched of men who were now marched the 15th	

WAR DIARY
or
INTELLIGENCE SUMMARY.

(Erase heading not required.)

Army Form C. 2148.

August 1917

Place	Date	Hour	Summary of Events and Information	Remarks and references to Appendices
	AUG 24th 1917	AM 2.25	That Guns were to open fire at SHAM FARM at 9.15 a.m. The bombardment of 2nd Corps barrage opening this at work was carried on by a General Barrage. Not Yet known. Fire continued here on until the BLACK LINE Forward position. Two Sections telephoned to by the Forward Observation Officer that Enemy was on the Objective and any counter attack. Our guns fired on BATTY KO trenches for the SOS Front Line. There was no reply to any enemy gun fire. 35 [?] The shelling was not heavy + our field cause delay with the mud and could not move up as rapidly as [?] the rear of the 15th RWKS, was shifty as most important many Germans were shewn to surrender and no one had any idea being hurried by the Enemy [?] and our own — The majority of the units seemed to come from the direction of ZONNEBEKE and N. W. and were from the SOUTH. the morning fog brought about a trouble what our Lines looked under their own guns. Returned	16 [?]

WAR DIARY
or
INTELLIGENCE SUMMARY

Army Form C. 2118.

Place	Date	Hour	Summary of Events and Information	Remarks and references to Appendices
	August 2nd 1917		Men were over the knees in water and falling in shell holes here & good many casualties from shell fire and snipers were busy in my own Co. I know owing at one time of three men buried to the armpits in BONS FARM trench and one great difficulty was with regard to the evacuation of the wounded. Many of the wounded lie out for 48 hours and rain & wind information provided. POMMERN REDOUBT & near arrived about 3.30 P.M. HARSHAW was about my right mid way on PLUM FARM so we stood 30 men very much day and night some wounded Stretcher bearers were working many had evacuations and the time of evacuation was upon us. Our few regimental stretcher bearers were knocked up extremely but the one of the wine one carrying in carried some some horse having officers and seen up . I did not know of POMMERN REDOUBT being used N. LEE'S Wd. Q.M. nunnery next to PLUM FARM & near	
		A.M. 9.15	the Arty were turn in the Barrage at 9.15 am and starts	

WAR DIARY or INTELLIGENCE SUMMARY

Army Form C. 2118.

Place	Date	Hour	Summary of Events and Information	Remarks and references to Appendices
	Aug 9th 1917		Hours to ... in glorious ... We were ... the Chief of Staff on a history. WALEN FARM and POMMERN REDOUBT very heavily and then ordnance came into their way. Slowly the ... orders given from the Brigade Signal ... however the information that the Germans had recaptured the BLACK LINE the very day. To recapture the BLACK LINE the very day. All units were sent up at 2.45 to hold on and to await the arrival of the 9th and 9/6 KRRC on the lost line. A second mopping up followed saying that the Brigade strong that is relieved. Receiving now more intimate news from the front line arrived in Jackson Trench with the men into dugouts and were hideously ... with CAPTAIN TRENCH a left command who walked ... men were ensured he ready to meet a counter-attack and to clean their rifles as well as they could. Major KING ...	
		MIDDAY		

WAR DIARY or INTELLIGENCE SUMMARY.

Army Form C. 2118.

(Erase heading not required.)

19 of [unclear] August 1917

Place	Date	Hour	Summary of Events and Information	Remarks and references to Appendices
	Aug 2nd 1917		Were bombing TONMEEN CASTLE on our right, [unclear] [unclear] to get into touch with our one on their right flank. It was not evident that the division on our right had reached its [unclear] came in that a Convoy [unclear] was [unclear] [unclear] of 3 [?] KNS [unclear] on its left flank — was [unclear]. On the eastern [unclear] [unclear] East of H4-35 — the [unclear] [unclear] [unclear] [unclear] [unclear] [unclear] at H4-7.7.9.2.7 —	
		P.M. 2.40	At 2-40 P.M. the enemy [unclear] [unclear] a [unclear] [unclear] [unclear] and a very [unclear] [unclear] [unclear] were [unclear] a demonstration [unclear] west of H4-35. The [unclear] [unclear] [unclear] [unclear] [unclear] of the heaviest sort by coming [unclear] [unclear] the front of the front [unclear] [unclear] [unclear] about 60 (sixty) strong, but was [unclear] [unclear] in front and the [unclear] of [unclear] coming [unclear] on very long on this [unclear] them [unclear] [unclear] [unclear] nearly [unclear] [unclear] [unclear] [unclear]	

WAR DIARY or INTELLIGENCE SUMMARY

Army Form C. 2118.

(Erase heading not required.)

Place: August 1917

Date	Hour	Summary of Events and Information	Remarks and references to Appendices
Aug 2nd 1917		Got our tots of rum - everyone was cheerful & in good spirits. We knew that we would win through up the sunken road. We soon found that rifles were quite useless owing to the mud on reaching our objective, we had to clear them. The Lewis guns worked better & no dugouts cleaned as well as no sporte under the darkness. The French who often had L.G.s changed. Lewis (?) rifles & rounds of ammunition & anyone that was wet and needed a cartridge firing. Machine Guns had been placed in any breach when the enemy immediately he appeared over Hill 35. It was clear that our chief hope survived in a counter attack but in view & in the support force. The enemy advanced but each time he was driven back, artillery fire before reaching the top of Hill 35. aided our watching beyond a few isolated parties. The German also kept up a very heavy barrage. It kept our home line and them back.	

WAR DIARY or INTELLIGENCE SUMMARY

Army Form C. 2118

(Erase heading not required.)

August 1917

Place	Date	Hour	Summary of Events and Information	Remarks and references to Appendices
FARM	Aug 2nd 1917		Recent received information of relief by 6 Yorkshires. The whole night by the 9th C.L.R. Relieving our horses as many of our dead as we could. Left in the evening. The relieving Battalion arrived about in the early morning. Our Lewis guns complete.	
	Aug 3rd		The Battalion marched back in small parties to CONGREVE WALK. Rain is still falling. Trenches and dug-outs exceedingly difficult to move. Col. Burgess with Bn. Sgt. and four have joined from the Citron. Had 16 hours rest for today. There was little if no sleep. The rain continued throughout the day and no orders arrived as to our further movements. A large number of our Lotterie had moved up to this Burgess, and the enemy bombarded Bascentain I believe in reprisals of NCW relief of 3 Bns. and now less prevalence all the morning. In the afternoon we received that we were to move up at	
		5 P.M.		

WAR DIARY or INTELLIGENCE SUMMARY

Army Form C. 2118.

(Erase heading not required.)

Place	Date	Hour	Summary of Events and Information	Remarks and references to Appendices
VLAMERTINGHE	Aug 3rd 1917		VLAMERTINGHE at 9.30 P.M. Back to WATOU by M.T. from the garrison sent to front. While we were there the enemy continued a constant shell fire with gas. The Brigade consisted of 3 Field Batteries many of them new arrivals who were sent into action straight away in support of their own troops also from New Zealand among a party of tired men.	
		8 P.M.	A line we relieved ran along just the Frezenberg switched and Garrigardly left POT-IZE in VLAMERTINGHE. The cookers left had haught to VLAMERTINGHE and then moved the connecting shore and the advance broke the Battalion Line a fairly strongly men who to the Hull attacks. A little movement of troops to hospital in No.1 Area a long line of huts was used to take the whole Brigade but there was no difficulty for a delay in taking snow covered was met by the prolonged in the dark.	
	Aug 4	10.30 a.m.	Battalion up at about 12-30 am and was on about to 3 Wounded away from the Fresh the Battalion broke about	

WAR DIARY or INTELLIGENCE SUMMARY

Army Form C. 2118.

(Erase heading not required.)

Place	Date	Hour	Summary of Events and Information	Remarks and references to Appendices
ABEELE	Aug 3rd 1917		On the road a bit. They could not start till march to Dickebush. Many of the men ended up with arab equipment at Dickebush old trek wrong mitroned — is one impossible to keep any orderly formation. It was pouring light steady rain the whole day.	
ABEELE	Aug 4th		Walked and viewed & waded for about 3 miles of the telephone message was not getting down to Bn in evening & day. The telephone message was wrong to the Bde from Brigade Guard Goad Mur. is the skies beneath of A [...] Brig Lt Knoyal Capt. Tried very hard and gallantly I up to [...] the men dying chiefly on the great and [...] fire [...] being the galleries are not ready for them in trenches and were helpful and a great help to relieve them in very bad way in which they suffered. The season was [...] run Company was very near many counter mate than a [...] stabbed in my Brigade (Signed) J. Bryan [...] Bipatie Pando [...]	
				R. Bryan Cap 4 TI 1917 I/M

WAR DIARY
or
INTELLIGENCE SUMMARY.

Army Form C. 2118.

Place	Date	Hour	Summary of Events and Information	Remarks and references to Appendices
ABEELE	AUG 4th 1917		The Battalion went out when with 16 Liverpool then over 566 the wounded finally was taken to the half way dressing room KILLED 44, WOUNDED 193.	
			MISSING 6. England where they form Kent FOREST en	
			KILLED 2nd Lieut HICKEY Died of wounds 2nd Lieut DEY	
			Remember missing 2nd Lieut RANDALL RAWCLIFFE	
ABEELE			WHITE and TOWLE were wounded 2nd Lieut HENRY wounded this have got 2nd Lieut ELAM Lieut K Hume Lt Klaunt and the scene of way into the arrangement Lieut LLOYD was down with pneumonia to go on as the Battalion Comr and if the trenches where relieved all which were on the to about 3 yds to the enemy and shelled heavy were very intense the Lewis gun though having some still fire the Lineman encroachent into the fire kept out repeatedly by sweeping fire the 31st men N.W. Costs while leaving at	
			W D GEAKE on Rtd as the 31st men N.W. Costs while leaving at	

WAR DIARY
or
INTELLIGENCE SUMMARY.

Army Form C. 2148.

23

Place	Date	Hour	Summary of Events and Information	Remarks and references to Appendices
ABEELE	Aug 5		The Divisional Commander came over in the morning & gave to the Brigade he intended to putting the Battalion through a scheme of Brigade in Mobile Offn. which he is carrying through himself. A Representative from their Division experienced.	
	Aug 6	9.30 am	G.O.C. Battalion Inspection by Offrs.	
		11.30 am	Station entrained at 9.30 a.m. in ABEELE & detrained at 1 p.m. in AUDRUICQ moving thence	
BLANC PIGNON		6.30 pm	Oct. Our Battalion reported to Brigade for BLANC PIGNON	
	8		2nd Lieut Grahame reported for duty from Command depot	
	9		and in Chas Bridges & 10 ors rants & Nco's wounded in Camp joined the 2nd I.B. Depot	
	10		Capt L.S. ELTON awarded the D.S.O.	
	13		Brigade Field day in the morning Gen. 2nd Lieut T.R. WINDLE rejoined class of 3rd Bn. WINGS	
	15		The Battalion proceeded to the Bombing Pit for practice	
	16		During the service	

WAR DIARY
or
INTELLIGENCE SUMMARY.
(Erase heading not required.)

Army Form C. 2118.

August 1917

Place	Date	Hour	Summary of Events and Information	Remarks and references to Appendices
BLANC PIGNON.	Aug 17		Battalion sent one N.C.O. & 3 men on a course of instruction to the R.O.D. Armed Guard Quarters at Follen during the afternoon.	
	18		The following promotions &c. to 2nd Lieut. F.B. PETERS, 2nd Lieut. A. W. NEWMAN, 2nd Lieut. R. SNEEZUM, 2nd Lieut. H. BRANDON and 2nd Lieut. A.W. RICHMAN of D Brigade R.G.A. were taken on the strength of the Battalion.	
	19		Ceremonial, Close Quarter drill, gas drill, etc. The Battalion were employed during the day in the training area.	
	21		Brigade Drawn day on training area.	
	24		List of Military Honors were awarded to following O.R.s of the Battalion during the Military Period — During the most of June—	
			A/CSM. MEADOWS J. — Cpl. CLARK T. — Pte. WESTWOOD W.P. — Pte. PARRY E.O.	
			Sgt. McCARTEN J. — L/Cpl. MARGRAVE J. — Pte. SHALLCROSS J.J. — BROUGH J.M.	
			" POPE W.T. — L/Sgt. LEWIS S. — " ROWLANDS R. — " MOTTRAM H.	
			L/Sgt. PENNINGTON T. — Sgt. SHAW W.H. — " ENTWISTLE W.J. — " McDOUGAL S.	
			AND, Sgt. GRIFFITH W, Sgt. WALKER R.D. and Pte. BENTLY L. received Meritorious Service Medals.	

WAR DIARY
or
INTELLIGENCE SUMMARY.
(Erase heading not required.)

Army Form C. 2118.

August 1917   19th The Kings Own Royal Regt 7F

Place	Date	Hour	Summary of Events and Information	Remarks and references to Appendices
BLANC PIGNON.	25.		2 O/R reported in reinforcements	
	26.		Brigadier General Gwyn M.C.? Over? Military review to be more? later but when the General to review the troops on roof? circle? the Battalion. B.M.	
			General Bartman? alone his car	
			The following General Wilson arrived by car from G.H.Q. 5th Army	
			TRANSPORT DRIVEN	
			The Army Commander recently mentioned that command in chief to proceed down in the new?	
			the General turning clutch on completion into the liberty ground	
			YPRES and more easily side? of country shown by the new gateway	
			from on the regiments of the Army through YPRES out	
			where near our new army line	
			The Belu? Maryland? considered it only round but to having considered it only towards the ruins in then	
			can comment on? I was surveyed? to drive in	
			Called: Division Commander by a dying Chief the Division	
			General ? who was looking forward to reverse? the Division	

A6945 Wt. W14422/M1160 350,000 12/16 D. D. & L. Forms/C./2118/14

Army Form C. 2118.

WAR DIARY
or
INTELLIGENCE SUMMARY.

(Erase heading not required.)

Place	Date	Hour	Summary of Events and Information	Remarks and references to Appendices
BLANC PIGNON	Aug 1917 28		22 o/R arrived to Company reinforcement	
	29		Promotion by officers are published the following the following officers are given the MILITARY CROSS. Lieut. T. D. HARRISON, 2nd Lieut. W.H. GELDERD, Capt. L.C.S. RICHER, and the following officers given a bar to their MILITARY CROSS Capt. E.H.G. ROBERTS M.C., 2nd Lieut S.H. RANDALL M.C. 1 D.C.M. also won by Pvnt. S. Foster No 33003.

Since coming out of the line the Battalion has been training the same line as at MORINGHEM. The training occupies some 4 hours a day and Saturday the remainder being in the vicinity of the huts and Sunday being an off day. Every one seems to be thoroughly enjoying themselves at present. On Sunday afternoon the Buglers of the Bn gave an enjoyable concert in a room at 1 P.M. after which the Rates or Banner is gave a return concert / attack 10 P.M. | |

Army Form C. 2118.

WAR DIARY
or
INTELLIGENCE SUMMARY.
(Erase heading not required.)

August 1917. 1/9 R. Irish Regt. Batt. T.F.

Place	Date	Hour	Summary of Events and Information	Remarks and references to Appendices
BLANC PIGNON.	AUG 28th 1917		Nothing occurred. The weather throughout the month has been changeable with some very hot days although no rify fine days. On the whole there has been fighting going on trying to push armies beyond the German lines where they are stronger than never.	
	AUG 31st		In the field. Sept 1st 1917. The following officers returned as missing :- 2nd Lieut BONIFACE, 2nd " ROBERTSON, 2nd " WALTON. T.F. 2nd " CATHER. R.A. 2nd " WARD. R.C. REEVES A.M. F M Dean Major Comdg 1/9 R Royal Irish T.F.	A.W.

A6945 Wt. W14422/M160 350,000 12/16 D. D. & L. Forms/C./2118/14.

CONFIDENTIAL

WAR DIARY

OF

1/9 LIVERPOOL R.

FOR PERIOD

1/9/17 – 30/11/17

WO 29 55/165

WAR DIARY
or
INTELLIGENCE SUMMARY.

Army Form C. 2118.

(Erase heading not required.)

September 1917 / 9. Batt^n. the King's (Liverpool Regt) T.F.

Place	Date	Hour	Summary of Events and Information	Remarks and references to Appendices
BLANC PIGNON	1st to 15th		During this period the weather was perfect except for a few days on which it rained somewhat heavily. The Battalion did the usual four hours daily training (in accordance with 5th Army Instructions issued in Bryan's Memorandum) Training was carried out on "The Nose" & "Strong Point" almost daily in "Companies" an Attack was a notable feature. The normal routine was also carried out. In addition "Classes for Officers" were taken by Major E.G. HOARE and "Instruction Lectures to N.C.O's" by R.S.M. also Training of Signallers, Snipers, Signallers & men their own programme carried out. Between this and the area was visited on three or four occasions by enemy aeroplanes. Be times chosen by them was apparent to be between 10 P.M. & 12 P.M. & a large number of bombs of a heavy type were dropped some falling near to the Billets occupied by the Battalion but without causing any casualties or much damage	SHEET 27/A FRANCE NE D.35 a 15.60 [signature] [signature]

Army Form C. 2118.

WAR DIARY
or
INTELLIGENCE SUMMARY. /9 Bath: the King Liverpool Regt
(Erase heading not required).

September 1919.

Place	Date	Hour	Summary of Events and Information	Remarks and references to Appendices
BLANC PIGNON	3rd		A Brigade field day was held on the 3rd and on the	
	4		10th a divisional day involving a visible failure being the	
			rest of the Commander-in-Chief & the General Officer Commanding	
			1st Army who inspected the work done in progress with keen interest	
	4		On this day 95% of the Battalion who were due for or required	K.S.
			inoculation were duly inoculated (178) by the Battalion Medical	
			Officer LIEUT G.W. HARRISON	K.S.
	6		The Division held their annual Horse Show, Gymkhana Sports	
			and extremely successful sports exhibition during the afternoon being	
			perfect but hot yet in a heavy downpour of rain during events to rather	
			an early close. This Battalion was very successful in the competition	
			provided, being 3rd in the aggregate number of points scored. In	
			events run by this Battalion we won two FIRSTS, two SECONDS, & two (2)	
			THIRDS, and also sensed FOURTH & FIFTH in two other events, a record	
			which must be regarded as very satisfactory as all the events concerned	
			reached a very high standard	K.S.

Army Form C. 2118.

WAR DIARY
or
INTELLIGENCE SUMMARY.
(Erase heading not required.)

1/9 Bdn Kings Loyal Regt 75

September 1917

Instructions regarding War Diaries and Intelligence Summaries are contained in F. S. Regs., Part II. and the Staff Manual respectively. Title pages will be prepared in manuscript.

Place	Date	Hour	Summary of Events and Information	Remarks and references to Appendices
BLANC PIGNON	1st to 15th		Owing this period of rest the Battalion had ample facilities for bathing the men. The Zone Allotment who are exceptionally good and the Billets arranged for all ranks were comfortable and of good class. The whole Brigade seemed quite refreshed a/c the 5 weeks rest and hoping by their experiences in having the area see ready Rfd for any further work which might be required of them. The Bttn. left BLANC PIGNON on the 15th marching to PUDRICQ where they entrained at 9.15 am arriving at PESELHOEK about 3.30 pm (The proceeded of the Transport moved by road on the 14th at 7 am) When the Battalion detrained, and marched to No 2, AREA.	W/O W/O W/O W/O SHEET NO. 28.N.W. BELGIUM
VLAMERTINGHE	15th		VLAMERTINGHE.	
	17th		This was an exceedingly busy day, which was spent in equipping the men in fighting order for the attack. About midday the enemy shelled the camp and his H.V. Gun but no damage was	

Army Form C. 2118.

WAR DIARY
or
INTELLIGENCE SUMMARY.
(Erase heading not required.)

1/9 Battn. King's Liverpool Rgt.

Month: September

Place	Date	Hour	Summary of Events and Information	Remarks and references to Appendices
VLAMERTINGHE	19th		None	
		7 P.M.	Commencing about 7 P.M. the Battalion left VLAMERTINGHE, Companies moving off independently, the order being A. B. C. D and H.Q. The Battalion went into action as follows:-	K.
			Commanding Officer Lieut. Colonel F.M. DREW	
			Second in Command A/Captain E.H.G. ROBERTS MC.	
			Adjutant 2nd Lieut C.B JOHNSON	
			Sig Officer 2nd Lieut N. LEES	
			Medical Officer Lieut A.W. HARRISON MC.	K.
			A Company. Captain ELTON. L.S. in command	
			2nd Lieut LUNNON W.J.	
			2nd Lieut BONIFACE W.H.	
			2nd Lieut BRYAN P.J.	
			B. Company. Captain A.G. WARDE MC.	K.
			2nd Lieut NEWMAN A	

WAR DIARY or INTELLIGENCE SUMMARY

Army Form C. 2118.

1/9 Bath. Kings Loyal Regt

September

Place	Date	Hour	Summary of Events and Information	Remarks and references to Appendices
			B Company 2nd Lieut J. ROBERTS	W.R.
			2nd Lieut T.F. WALTON	
			C Company Captain R.O. WILDE MC. in command	W.R.
			2nd Lieut A.W. RICHMAN	
			2nd Lieut C.W. HAMILTON-JONES	
			2nd Lieut O.A.V. SEELES	
			D Company 2nd Lieut A.M. ADAMS in command	W.R.
			2nd Lieut HOSKYN J.H.	
			2nd Lieut T.P. CAIRNS	
			2nd Lieut R.O. WARD	
			2nd Lieut R. SNEEZUM	
			Headquarters Detach. M/R/M D. ROBERTS	W.R.
			Sgt. THOMPSON	
			TOTAL STRENGTH OF BATTALION :- OFFICERS 22	W.R.
			OTHER RANKS 514 / 536	

Army Form C. 2118.

WAR DIARY
or
INTELLIGENCE SUMMARY. 1/9 Battn Kings Own Royal Regt
(Erase heading not required.)

Instructions regarding War Diaries and Intelligence Summaries are contained in F. S. Regs., Part II. and the Staff Manual respectively. Title pages will be prepared in manuscript.

Month: September

Place	Date	Hour	Summary of Events and Information	Remarks and references to Appendices
	19th		The Companies marched along the main road to YPRES and found that the road was exceedingly congested with traffic of all kinds. At the WATER TOWER they turned to the LEFT, crossed the PLAINE D'AMOUR passed the DIXMUDE GATE and proceeded along W.S. TRACK to the OLD BRITISH FRONT LINE.	
			A & B Companies took up a position in the OLD GERMAN FRONT LINE close to the intersection of that line by W.S. TRACK and made use of the remaining German "Pillboxes". C & D Companies took up a position in the OLD BRITISH FRONT LINE — in this place they were somewhat congested as there was not much DUGOUT accommodation. Latterly it was a fine night and the enemy did not offer on account of the weather. Casualties were sustained in WARWICK FARM DUGOUT where also were the Headquarters of the 9th Kings Own Battalion. relieved the 1/5 South Lancashire Regiment 7.F and the 1/5 the Kings Own Royal Lancaster Regt. of the 165.	

WAR DIARY or INTELLIGENCE SUMMARY

Army Form C. 2118.

1/9 Bttn. King's Liverpool Regt. T.F.

September 1917

Place	Date	Hour	Summary of Events and Information	Remarks and references to Appendices
Infantry Brigade.	17		The move was accomplished without casualties as there was very little hostile shelling. Dispositions were taken up and the Battalion reported "Relief Complete" at 1.0 AM. During the day there was nothing as worth as possible. About	
	18	5 PM.	the Divisional Commander interviewed the Commanding officer at B.H.Q. WARWICK FARM. Between 7.15 pm and 8.0 pm A&B Coys moved up to the then BRITISH FRONT LINE, B Coy taking up a position between SOMME & POMMERN with B.H.Q. at SOMME. A Coy was accommodated at BANK FARM. C & D Coys took over the position in the GERMAN FRONT LINE vacated by A & B Coys. H.Q. left WARWICK FARM at 7.15 PM & experienced some difficulty in reaching BANK FARM as the Guide lost his way. The enemy Artillery on the STEENBEKE Valley for a heavy barrage. No casualties were sustained.	

WAR DIARY
or
INTELLIGENCE SUMMARY. 1/9 Hastings 1500 Regt.

Army Form C. 2118.

Place	Date	Hour	Summary of Events and Information	Remarks and references to Appendices
	19th		The Battalion relieved the 1/5 South Lancs Regt. and then held the line - this was an exceedingly busy day in making final arrangements for the attack. At 7.30 PM "C" & "D" Companies moved up into the front line - the night was exceptionally dark & rain commenced to fall at 10-45 PM. Capt. A.G. WAROE MC & Lt. Williams were detailed to tape out an assembly line - it is proper to remark that the 55th Division relieved by us not left a continuous front line. After about 2 hours had been heard from Capt. WAROE and shortly before midnight Capt. ROBERTS M.C. & L/Cpl GILL went to SOMME and reconnoitred the ground between SOMME and POMMERN but did not find him.	
	20		At 1.5 AM. Captain WAROE returned and reported that he had marked out our jumping off line but had been forced to get in touch with the 9th Kings on our right	

Army Form C. 2118.

WAR DIARY
or
INTELLIGENCE SUMMARY.   1/9 the Kings Footety

(Erase heading not required.)

Instructions regarding War Diaries and Intelligence Summaries are contained in F. S. Regs., Part II. and the Staff Manual respectively. Title pages will be prepared in manuscript.

September

Place	Date	Hour	Summary of Events and Information	Remarks and references to Appendices
	20.		At 4.45 AM the Battalion was reported to be in position ready for the attack and about this time the enemy put down a barrage of 150 MM. and 105 MM on the line SOMME - POMMERN. At 5.5 am Lieut Colonel DREW left BANK FARM for SOMME to conduct operations. Before going in to active operations it is well to mention that the enemy was employing the new system of defence in by the 2nd Guards Reserve division which consisted of the 15th, the 91st and the 91st Reserve Infantry Regiments. The garrison zone of the YPRES group of the 4th German Army. The enemy did not hold a continuous front line but had placed short garrisons & clumps of machine guns with enfilading arcs of fire in the strongly connected "pill boxes" which were echeloned in depth. This was a new system of defence adopted by the enemy as a counter measure to the British new formation of attack. Zero was at	
		5.28	At 5.28. AM hostile shelling increased.	A.R.

WAR DIARY or INTELLIGENCE SUMMARY

Army Form C. 2118.

(Erase heading not required.)

19. The Kings Liverpool Regt

Month and year: September

Place	Date	Hour	Summary of Events and Information	Remarks and references to Appendices
	20.	5-40 AM	at which time the heavier field guns & machineguns opened fire. The Battalion advanced in 4 waves (each Company forming one wave) in the following order B, A, C, D. The distance between waves was 50 yards. The Battalion on the right was held up at LENS for several minutes, the left of the Battalion being at the same time able to advance in the direction of GAVRELOT. At LENS rifle grenades were used against the enemy who were in the open, and under cover of these rifle grenades the men were able to advance by short rushes from shell crater to shell crater so that eventually our men approached so close to the strong point that one & two were able to creep round the flanks whilst others approached from the front. The garrison then surrendered & about 30 prisoners were taken.	
In 9 Rd/kt opp.			In support of the Battalion was open lower up at Hill 35 and it was not until the 6th Kings came up & reinforced the	

Army Form C. 2118.

WAR DIARY
or
INTELLIGENCE SUMMARY.
(Erase heading not required.)

1/9 Bn. The Kings Liverpool Regt

September

Place	Date	Hour	Summary of Events and Information	Remarks and references to Appendices
			The Battalion Halt any leading could be made. The left of the Battalion proceeded on to the lounge and took a strong point which consisted of a block house in the LEFT Battalion boundary about 150 yards to the NORTH of GALLIPOLI then taking 2 Machine Guns killing all the garrison. Capt. R.C. WILDE MC then led the attack on GALLIPOLI where the opposition was strong and determined — the enemy withheld his fire until our men were about 60 yards away when he opened fire with 2 Machine Guns, despite this our men were able to advance under cover of rifle grenades from Steel crabs until they got to GALIPOLI where a violent hand to hand encounter took place and it is pleasing to note that the dugouts was freely used, the garrison eventually surrendering after suffering very heavy casualties, and four Machine Guns & about 30 prisoners were taken. Captain R.C. WILDE then consolidated his headquarters at GALIPOLI and relieved his men	

Army Form C. 2118.

WAR DIARY
or
INTELLIGENCE SUMMARY.
(Erase heading not required.)

1/9 Batt. The King's Lpool Regt T.F.

Place	Date	Hour	Summary of Events and Information	Remarks and references to Appendices
Havrincourt	20		The Commanding Officer was on a return of the Reconnaissance men of his Battalion from SOMME & later on GARROU and at noon he returned to Battalion Head Quarters at BANK FARM having a thorough grasp of the situation. A few minutes before his arrival the Signallers had succeeded by heroic effort in establishing Telephonic Communication with Brigade. This enabled the Commanding Officer to confer with the Brigadier whom he informed that until Battalion 4) of the 1/5 South Lancs Regt. were gone in near Lieut Colonel Evans' command. He motioned to give to these Companies when they came up about 2 hours afterwards orders to capture and consolidate Hill 37. About this time it was reported that the Commanding Officer of the 1/5 Lpool was seriously wounded whereupon the	15/8

WAR DIARY
or
INTELLIGENCE SUMMARY.

(Erase heading not required.)

Army Form C. 2118.

1/9 Hastings Essex Regt T.F.

September 1917

Place	Date	Hour	Summary of Events and Information	Remarks and references to Appendices
	20.		Commanding Officer of this Brigade was given primary power over the left sector of the Brigade in which was included also ~~RANDALL~~ WH the 5th Loyal North Lancashire Regiment.	
			About 5 PM a message was received from Brigade that men were seen retiring from Hill 35 and Captain E.H.G. ROBERTS and R.S.M. ROBERTS were detailed to go there and rally the men and recovery. They found all the men on Hill 35 and at LENS and GALIPOLI, manfully & cheerfully standing to their post.	
			Shortly afterwards at about 7 PM the enemy launched a heavy counter attack which was broken up by our artillery and machine gun fire and not a single man retired	

Army Form C. 2118.

WAR DIARY
or
INTELLIGENCE SUMMARY. 1/9 The Kings (Liverpool) Regt
(Erase heading not required.)

September 1917

Place	Date	Hour	Summary of Events and Information	Remarks and references to Appendices
			During the night of the 20/21st two (2) Companies of the 10th Kings (Scottish) Regt were placed at Lewis Lodge area and these to detailed to protect our left flank of the Brigade front at ELM CORNER. The night passed quietly but	
Zillebeke	21		about 9 P.M. the 21st a hostile aeroplane flew over the vicinity of BANK FARM dropping several very lights. The remainder of the day was fairly quiet and we continued our work and were done. The Commanding Officer reorganizing the Lewis Gun areas arranging for a being detailed for each area.	
			About 4 P.M. Brigade sent a message that a counter attack was imminent and were to point in the direction one naming to "STAND TO" – about 6.45 P.M. a very counter attack was launched but owing to the magnificent barrage put down by our Artillery & Machine Guns the enemy was unable to penetrate our line, about 9 P.M. the situation	

WAR DIARY
INTELLIGENCE SUMMARY

Army Form C. 2118.

1/9 Hastings Zouave Regt.

September 1917

Place	Date	Hour	Summary of Events and Information	Remarks and references to Appendices
	22.		became normal and dispositions as before owing to the splendid organisation of R.S.M Roberts all units in the LEFT Sector were supplied with RATIONS, WATER, BOMBS, S.A.A. The day was strongly quiet, and much useful work was done in laying tracks to POMMERN and SOMME, and establishing an advanced DUMP at SOMME. During the morning the Brigade Major rode BANK FARM and arranged final details for the relief of the LEFT sector by the 59th Division and operation orders were issued to the various units under Lieut Colonel Dawes Command. The night was exceptionally quiet and the relief took place in a most orderly manner, and was able to report to Brigade that "RELIEF COMPLETE" by 2.20 a.m on the morning of the 23rd	
	23.		The cohering effect No reluctant Conduct of the operations and mention must be made as to the efficiency of the medical arrangements to dividing gallantly of the St. Bn. Bearers who worked with the utmost devotion	

WAR DIARY
or
INTELLIGENCE SUMMARY

Army Form C. 2118.

1/9 Batt. Kings Liverpool Regt.

September 1917

Place	Date	Hour	Summary of Events and Information	Remarks and references to Appendices
	23		and succeeded in extricating the wounded in a remarkably short space of time. The Battalion Runners acquitted themselves with courage fortitude and their alacrity and cheerfulness throughout the whole situation during which they had many dangerous and difficult missions to perform are worthy of remark. Orders	
			The Battalion rendezvoused at VLAMERTINGHE No 2 AREA where a hot meal was awaiting them.	
		20-22	The disposition of the Battalion was in the left sector under Lieut Colonel D'Urso Command were as follows:—	
			9ᵗʰ & Cᵗʰ KINGS L(Pool) REST. GALLIPOLI SEVEN HILL 35 with a few advanced posts.	
			1/5ᵗʰ L. NORTH LANCS. KIER FARM Dugouts, and protecting front	
			of HILL 35.	
			1/5 SOUTH LANCS. HILL 37.	
			2 Coys 1/10 L(Pool) (SCOTTISH) Protecting Left Flank from KIER FARM	

Army Form C. 2118.

WAR DIARY
or
INTELLIGENCE SUMMARY.
(Erase heading not required.)

9 Bttn Durham Light Inf. September 1917

Place	Date	Hour	Summary of Events and Information	Remarks and references to Appendices
VLAMERTINGHE	23		The Battalion entrained at VLAMERTINGHE at 11-30 a.m. proceeded to POPERINGHE detrained about 12 noon & proceeded by route march to the WATOU Area arriving about 3 P.M.	
	24		The Companies were for the next two days occupied at the disposal of Company Commanders for reorganization, cleaning up,	
	25		refitting of equipment & refitting.	
	26		The Battalion paraded at 8. AM & marched to PESELHOEK entraining there at 11-30 A.M. and proceeded to BAPAUME & the troops detrained about 9 P.M. & then marched to the BARASTRE	
BAPAUME			AREA arriving there about 11 P.M.	
BARASTRE AREA	27 28		For the three following days the Companies were again placed at the disposal of the Company Commanders to complete refitting & reorganization.	
	29 30		Boxing Competitions were held every day under keen competition. The Battalion marched to the front line the scene of contest, but were following an early dusk crossed the final ponts to hot-spoors	

D. H. & L. London, E.C.
(A-853) Wt. W29/M.672 350,000 4/17 Ech. 52a Forms C/2118/4

Army Form C. 2118.

WAR DIARY
or
INTELLIGENCE SUMMARY.
(Erase heading not required.)

1/5 East Surrey [Regt] T.F.

September 1917

Place	Date	Hour	Summary of Events and Information	Remarks and references to Appendices
	30		The following reinforcements arrived during the month:-	
			1st Second Lieut. F.J. BRAGG. 3rd Devonshire Regt.	
			11th 68 other Ranks	
			17th 91 other Ranks	
			19th 2 other Ranks	
			28th 2 other Ranks	
			30th Second Lieut Wheeler seconded 3rd Kings.	
			The following CASUALTIES were unfortunately sustained during the operations of the 20/23rd Sept	
			Sec. Lieut. A. NEWMAN KILLED	
			" HAMILTON-JONES C.N. Capt. L.S. ELTON WOUNDED	
			" HOSKYN J.W. Capt. A.G. WARDE "	
			" JEEVES C.A.V. Sec. Lieut. J. ROBERTS "	
			" ADAMS Mc. AM. DIED OF WOUNDS " T.A. CAIRNS "	
			" BRAGG F.J. " R. SNEEZUM "	
			" A.W. RICHMAN "	
			" W.H. BONIFACE "	
			" W.J. LUNNON "	

Army Form C. 2118.

WAR DIARY
or
INTELLIGENCE SUMMARY.
(Erase heading not required.)

1/9 (Bath.) King's Liverpool Regt. T.F.

September 1917

Place	Date	Hour	Summary of Events and Information	Remarks and references to Appendices
BARASTRE AREA	30		and the following of Ranks KILLED 26 DIED OF WOUNDS 5 WOUNDED 190 MISSING 44 TOTAL 265 In the field 3/10/17 F.M. Shaw Lt Col Lieut Colonel Commanding 1/9 Kings (Liverpool Regt) T.F. Congratulatory message attached.	

55th (WEST LANCASHIRE) DIVISION ORDER OF THE DAY.

The following telegrams from the V Corps have been received :-

"The Commander-in-Chief visited Corps Headquarters this evening and expressed himself very pleased in the work of both Divisions and sends them his congratulations and thanks".

"Fifth Army wire begins aaa Please congratulate 55th Division on the gallant defence of HILL 37 yesterday and upon the energy and resource displayed by Commanders on the spot in organising counter attacks aaa Ends aaa".

55th Division H.Q.,
23rd September, 1917.

Lieut-Colonel,
General Staff, 55th Division.

55th (WEST LANCASHIRE) DIVISION.
****

ORDER OF THE DAY.

The following telegram has been received from GENERAL SIR HERBERT PLUMER G.C.M.G., G.C.V.O., K.C.B., commanding the Second Army :-

"GENERAL JEUDWINE, Commanding 55th Division.

Many congratulations to you and your Division on your success yesterday aaa You must have accounted for a great many

GENERAL PLUMER."

55th Division H.Q.
22nd September, 1917.

Lieut-Colonel,
General Staff, 55th Division,

55th (WEST LANCASHIRE) DIVISION ORDER OF THE DAY.

1. The following telegrams have been received :-

"Fifth Army wire begins aaa The Army Commander wishes to thank all arms and all ranks for their splendid efforts in todays battle aaa Co-operation between Infantry Artillery and Flying Corps has been excellent and very important successes have been gained all along the front aaa Ends aaa".

"Corps Commander thanks Field and Heavy Artillery for their good work and the F.O.Os for the very useful and timely information sent in aaa Ends aaa".

"Corps Commander congratulates 9th and 55th Divisions and thanks them for their success today aaa Ends aaa".

2. The Major General Commanding wishes to add his thanks and congratulations to all arms and ranks of the Division.

There is no doubt whatever that in addition to making a very substantial advance over difficult ground stubbornly defended, well organized, and liberally provided with strong cover, artillery, and machine guns, the Division, aided most ably by the Corps Heavy Artillery, succeeded in dealing the enemy a very heavy blow, and causing him severe losses.

Success was due to the fine determination shown by all ranks and the hearty co-operation of Artillery, Engineers, Infantry, Machine Gun Companies, Trench Mortars and R.A.M.C. with each other, which is the sign of a united and disciplined Division.

(sd) T. ROSE PRICE.

55th Division H.Q.,
21st September 1917.

Lieut-Colonel.
General Staff, 55th Division.

55TH (WEST LANCASHIRE) DIVISION.

ORDER OF THE DAY.

The following telegram has been received from The Right Honourable E.G.V. Earl of DERBY, K.G., G.C.V.O., C.B., Secretary of State for War :-

"GENERAL JEUDWINE, 55th Division Hdqrs. B.E.F.

Well done 55th West Lancashire Divn accept my most hearty congratulations I sincerely trust your losses are not heavy

DERBY."

T. Rose Price.

55th Division H.Q.
24th September, 1917.

Lieut-Colonel,
General Staff, 55th Divn.

CONFIDENTIAL

Vol 30

War Diary
of
119th Lanc: R
for the period
1st to 31st October 1917

Army Form C. 2118.

WAR DIARY
or
INTELLIGENCE SUMMARY.

(Erase heading not required.)

1/9 Bn. The King's Liverpool Regt.

October 1917

Place	Date	Hour	Summary of Events and Information	Remarks and references to Appendices
AIZECOURT- -Le- Bas.	Oct 1st		The Battalion paraded at 9.30 am & proceeded by route march to AIZECOURT-LE-BAS, arriving at about 4.30pm, dinners being carried to the troops en route. On the 2nd inst. the Battalion paraded at 2.30pm	
ST. EMILIE.	2nd to 6th		& proceeded by route march to ST. EMILIE, arriving there about 4.30pm relieving 17 Bn. ROYAL SCOTS, in reserve. The billets in this area were in some sort of repair, the vicinity of the Camp was in a dilapidated condition, necessitating a fair amount of labour being spent in remaining debries (grenades & machinery). The usual working parties were turned to Sanitary & R.E. employ, during our stay in this Camp. Ample bathing facilities were provided for the men. The Battalion left ST. EMILIE on the 7th inst. Companies	
L'EMPIRE.	7th		marching on dependently stating about 10am proceeded to L'EMPIRE SECTOR (Left Battn. of R.I.G.T. Br.I.69D5.) Front Line relieving 1/6 KINGS. The enemy artillery during our	
OBS[THOR?] Captn[?]			stay in this Sector was very moderate except on occasions	

WAR DIARY or INTELLIGENCE SUMMARY

Army Form C. 2118.

(Erase heading not required.) 1st Bn. Wellington Regiment

October 1917

Place	Date	Hour	Summary of Events and Information	Remarks and references to Appendices
LEOPARD	7th 8th 9th		When in Sherwood Section Headquarters with 7/mds. A great amount of work was improved in the trenches at both HQrs. Elephant dugouts being erected. Trench drainage, & revetting of fire bays. On 10/10/17 mal Lieutenant Colonel Evers Rodmer commanding 1/65 Auckland Brigade Vice Brig-Gen W. Braithwaite CMG on leave. The usual patrols were sent out nightly but on no occasion were the enemy encountered. The weather during this period was rather dull & misty, with occasional showers of rain. On the night 12/13th the Battalion was relieved in the sector by the 16th (North) Bn. King's (Liverpool) Regt. & proceeded to anti-tank defence of the 1st BRIGADE relieving 1/10 (Scottish) Bn King's (Liverpool) Regt. relief being completed about 2 am 13 inst. An	
ADELPHI			In the Decavois sector, a deal of work was performed nightly under R.E. supervision in strongpoints, revetting, the erecting of dugouts, on the 16th inst. the Army Commander	

WAR DIARY
or
INTELLIGENCE SUMMARY
(Erase heading not required.)

October 1917. Of The King's (Liverpool) Regt.

Army Form C. 2118.

Place	Date	Hour	Summary of Events and Information	Remarks and references to Appendices
ADELPHI	17th		Visited the Companies in the line. The usual patrols were sent out nightly, & on two of these occasions the enemy were observed patrolling in large numbers.	
	18th		Lieut. Colonel N.O.N. Dreux rejoined the Battalion on 12th inst. & assumed command. The Battalion was relieved in the line on night of 17/18th by 1/7 Bn The King's (Nool) Regt. & proceeded to Vaughans.	
VAUGHAN'S BANK	18th		Supported in with H.Q. mainly at VAUGHAN'S BANK. 3 Companies in the line, & 1 in Vanguard. Practically the whole Battn. were engaged on various working parties. As Bn. Headquarters the work consists chiefly in demolishing about 40 huts & erecting strong & secure covers in their place. This formed the majority of the work in this sect.	
	22nd		On the 22nd inst., the Battalion was relieved by 15 King's Own, & proceeded by Light Railway to HAMEL.	
HAMEL	22nd		15 King's Own & proceeded by Light Railway to HAMEL, in Divisional Reserve, the men being accommodated in	

WAR DIARY or INTELLIGENCE SUMMARY

Army Form C. 2118.

/9 Bn The Kings (Liverpool) Regt

October 1917

Place	Date	Hour	Summary of Events and Information	Remarks and references to Appendices
HAMEL	22nd to 31st		Billets. The first day was spent in cleaning up & taking up incidents. The usual parade hours & programme of training were carried out consisting of "Handling of Arms", Bayonet fighting, Physical Training, Musketry, Firing on Ranges, Lewis Gun Instruction, Training of Snipers, Spacing, Classes in Map Reading for Junior Officers, Lectures & demonstrations in "Wiring, Bombing, Firing of Rifle Grenades & Shooting". A notable piece of work was performed by the unit e.g. the erection of a miniature Rifle Range. On the 29th inst. the Brig. Engr. Commanding inspected A. Company of the unit & in various schemes was carried out Storing Point. The Brigade Boxing Tournament was held on 30th inst. Several of our men being Competitors. The leave during the preceding 4 weeks was fair & good, & during the latter part of the month the	

Army Form C. 2118.

WAR DIARY
or
INTELLIGENCE SUMMARY.
(Erase heading not required.)

1/9 Bn. The King's (Liverpool Rgt)
October 1917.

Place	Date	Hour	Summary of Events and Information	Remarks and references to Appendices
HAMEL	2/10		Allotment was especially incurred.	
	6/10		The Battalion received the following	
			reinforcements during the present tour:-	
			Sep. 30. 2nd Lieut. WHEELER. F. 3rd Kings. Oct. 20th 2nd Lieut. BAKER. R. K. 3rd Kings	
			Oct. 10th 2nd Lieut. ENGLAND. C.R. 16th " " " 2nd Lieut. MULLINER. W. 2nd "	
			" " Lieut. RINGHAM. F.S. 16th " " " 2nd Lieut. WILSON. N. 9th "	
			" " Lieut. PROVOST. D. 10th " 1.30. 2nd Lieut. TENDER. J.H. 7th "	
			" 19th 2nd Lieut. EDMONDS. G.H. 9 Kings.	
			" " 2nd Lieut. NICHOLS. H.G. 9th "	
			" 22nd 2nd Lieut. YOUNG. F.W. 9th " The undermentioned Officers	
			" " 2nd Lieut. CRUIKS. F.G. 3rd " proceeded on leave during the	
			" " 2nd Lieut. WILLIAMS. G.P. 3rd " month:-	
			" " 2nd Lieut. KENNEDY. J.O.N. 3rd " Lieut. G.W. Harrison R.A.M.C.	
			" " 2nd Lieut. COLLINGS. L. 2nd " Capt. R.C. Aneele	
			" " 2nd Lieut. THORPE. H.G. 3rd " Lt Col. Thomasens	
			" " 2nd Lieut. WHITLOCK. C.B. 3rd " Capt. A.H.A. Picker	
				Lieut. H. Lees

WAR DIARY
or
INTELLIGENCE SUMMARY.

Army Form C. 2118.

(Erase heading not required.)

October 1917

Place	Date	Hour	Summary of Events and Information	Remarks and references to Appendices
HAMEL	27th		The following Officers were struck off strength of the unit having proceeded to England for 2 months tour of duty:—	
			Capt. F. Ashman	
			Capt. & Adjt. W. Paine M.C.	
			2nd Lieut. C.B. Johnson appointed to a/Capt. & a/Adjt. vice Capt. W. Paine M.C., 18/10/9/17.	
	31/10/17		The Battalion sustained the following casualties during the month:— 3. O.Ranks wounded (i.o. duty)	

C.G. Hoar Major. Commanding
1/9 The King's Liverpool Regt.

31.10.1917

165/55

War History
of the
19th Australian
Light Horse
Regiment
1st Sept November
1917

Confidential

5.5 Div A.Q

Herewith War Diary of KLR up to the time of leaving the Division

A Boyd Moss
B. General
14/8/16 Cdg 165 Inf Bde

WAR DIARY / INTELLIGENCE SUMMARY

Army Form C. 2118.

Place	Date	Hour	Summary of Events and Information	Remarks and references to Appendices
Trenches in front of The Knoll	18/9/11		Batt relieved 16th King's Liverpool in THE BIRDCAGE by Rifle Brigade.	
	19/9	10 p.m.	1 Killed & 3 Wounded whilst carrying out working party Dummy Trench. Fires in front of Interlaced Wire. They were eventually blown in about position.	
	20/9	6.20am	164 Brigade attacked Guillemont Farm & The Knoll. On completion with the operation the 10th King's Liverpool worked Dummy Trench in rear. "B" Coy and two men of "D" Coy no casualties. "A" and "C" Coys fresh at position on THE BIRDCAGE. East of the Path which lies from FLEECALL to EGO.	
			Hostilities throughout the day practically Nil.	
	21/9		Enemy Batteries worked at Dawn with Red & white Bay Mirror at Brushy Drummy Tench & Ignes ... in "C" & "D" lines	
	22/9		Batt HQrs Intre moved up to OSSUS WOOD to question line. Party returned from "B" line, Dawn & duty. No movement from the front line.	
			Reorganisation of our front line.	
	23/9	10.30	Batt relieved by 14th K.R.R. & proceeded to uneven billets in EMPIRE	

Army Form C. 2118.

WAR DIARY
or
INTELLIGENCE SUMMARY.
(Erase heading not required.)

Instructions regarding War Diaries and Intelligence Summaries are contained in F. S. Regs., Part II. and the Staff Manual respectively. Title pages will be prepared in manuscript.

Place	Date	Hour	Summary of Events and Information	Remarks and references to Appendices
	night of 12th Nov		Battn moved up from INCOURT by light Railway & relieved the 4th Battn Royal North Lancs in Left Battn (Right Brigade) Sector of THE BIRDCAGE.	
	14th to 5th		Vaux Patrols. The Battn Pioneers assisted in large dugout on the LEMPIRE ROAD North of Bn H.Q. and Bunk accommodation for 15 men. Men continually improving our emergency aid Post. During 5th evening 200 men of large number of T.M.'s harassing men & teams & Light Rly lines to West of Battn H.Q. Details 1 B. Coy formed "Ha-Ha" and "B-" Battn to west with Details of Park Coy & "C" Coy. Eagle Quarry!	
	6th		Heavy T.M. activity. Two of our men hit by ? actions.	
	7th		Sent killed by T.M. Enemy co-operation and movement BIRDCAGE & him. Enemy retaliation NIL.	
	8th		Two shells reported early. Enemy harassed M.T.M. Proceeded to Brigade Reserve @ EMPIRE.	
	night 10/11		The whole of the Battalion entrained from 12/11 to 17/11 was overtired in	

Army Form C. 2118.

WAR DIARY
or
INTELLIGENCE SUMMARY.
(Erase heading not required.)

Instructions regarding War Diaries and Intelligence Summaries are contained in F. S. Regs., Part II. and the Staff Manual respectively. Title pages will be prepared in manuscript.

Place	Date	Hour	Summary of Events and Information	Remarks and references to Appendices
	23/11		Bat. Batld @ LEMPIRE.	
	24/11		Issued Bivouac Working Party	
	25/11 to		ditto.	
	29/11			
	Night of 29/11		Bat. ordered to stand to from last evening @ 2am as enemy was expected to attack.	
	30/11		Enemy attack took place & see details attached hereto.	

Army Form C. 2118.

WAR DIARY
or
INTELLIGENCE SUMMARY.
(Erase heading not required.)

Instructions regarding War Diaries and Intelligence Summaries are contained in F. S. Regs., Part II. and the Staff Manual respectively. Title pages will be prepared in manuscript.

Place	Date	Hour	Summary of Events and Information	Remarks and references to Appendices
GUILLEMONT FARM	Nov 30th		On this day the 105th Infantry Brigade was holding from GUILLEMONT FARM to CATELET ROAD in the EMPIRE SECTOR. The 7th K.R.Rs were on the right, holding the GUILLEMONT FARM Subsector, the 8th K.R.Rs the centre subsector comprising ECO FLEE-ELIOLL and GRAFTON POSTS and the 1st K.R.Rs held the left subsector comprising the BIRDCAGE. The 9th K.R.Rs were in support to the whole Brigade. On the left flank of the Brigade was the 16th Infy Brigade & it had been reported that the 183 Infy Brigade was holding the enemy line. The disposition of the Batt" were:- A+D Coys were in Landing Alley & hadn't an dug out on the temporis Rd. B Coy distributed over the three Strong Points - Pekin - York - Empire East Tenks. Battn HQ were in Empire. Information had been received the day before that an enemy attack was imminent & 5 am the Batt" stood to arms at 5 am at the time every one was wearie. About 7-15am the enemy commenced a heavy	
	7-15am			

WAR DIARY
or
INTELLIGENCE SUMMARY.
(Erase heading not required.)

Army Form C. 2118.

Place	Date	Hour	Summary of Events and Information	Remarks and references to Appendices
	21/4/17	7.15 am	Bombardment of the enemy's posts using Rum-n-ephio Bomb against the BIRDCAGE. Heavy trench shells against the supporting points in rear including Batt HQ & also Gas Shells with Phosphorus Incendiary & Mustard Oil. What were fired at all targets. After a bombardment of about 20 Minutes the enemy attacked & captured the BIRDCAGE and VOLT BANK. His further advance in to 2 guide holes were arrested by the 6th KRR who held out in Keithley & Currington Posts & the 5th KRB who in Eristor & Bleckhall Posts inflicted Sanguinary losses on the enemy. The Infantry were unfortunately overcome. The enemy occupied RIDDLE, LIMERICK & NEATH Posts. He was able to continue his advance almost to the village of EPEHY. It is supposed that after being held up at Currington Post he formed a defensive flank along STONE LANE the enemy of the situation had not appeared from the [following] the Enemy	

Army Form C. 2118.

WAR DIARY
or
INTELLIGENCE SUMMARY.
(Erase heading not required.)

Place	Date	Hour	Summary of Events and Information	Remarks and references to Appendices
	30/11/17	7.15	were occupying. The gas alarm had been given & reserving message were sent to the Bde HQ & from Bde Cav to outhers. Various rumours began to come through.	
		9.30 a	About 9.30 a.m. the E.S.O. 2 of the Bde Hqrs arrived at Batt HQ & explained that the BRIDGE had been lost & that the enemy had broken through on the left & having was sent to Cav that a dismounted Bde of cavalry would take over the Batt sector, that Cav O were to hold themselves in readiness for counter-attack.	
		11.0 a	About 11.0 a.m. the C.O. went forward & selected a line along which "B" dug a trench to protect the North side of Templeux. He pointed then out to the Coy Commander + 2i/c. Coy immediately commenced to dig by about 2 hours "A" & "D" Coys had got well down. This work was somewhat impeded by a squadron of about a dozen low flying enemy planes which kept circling around Templeux to	

WAR DIARY
or
INTELLIGENCE SUMMARY.
(Erase heading not required.)

Army Form C. 2118.

Place	Date	Hour	Summary of Events and Information	Remarks and references to Appendices
	30/11	11.0 a.m.	When as they stopped they 2/5 Lower Fusiliers arrived at Lempire took up a position along the Lempire–Epéhy Road flanking the G.H.Q.line on the left. Officers of the 2 Lancers & 6 mounted Cavalry Rifles then arrived at H.Q. They were making arrangements to take over from this Batt when they were withdrawn. Never Officers of the 8th Queen's reported they had been sent up as supports in the Lempire sector.	
	30/11	1.30 p.m.	About 1.30 pm Lebon was detailed to go & occupy PRIEL CUTTING with Lindung by a picket of 2/N.Wheeler & 5 men to wanuive No 13 copse & Priel Cutting Lebon left for Priel Cutting upon 2:30 pm proceeding via Manure Crop Road & moving to enemy aerial activity the advance two to in artillery formation up to N°17 Copse. When they halted. My flank reserved word by the enemy	

WAR DIARY
or
INTELLIGENCE SUMMARY.
(Erase heading not required.)

Army Form C. 2118.

Place	Date	Hour	Summary of Events and Information	Remarks and references to Appendices
	30/11/17	5:30 p	and the Coy then took up a position plug in	
			About 5:30 pm "B" Coy was ordered to reinforce 6 KRR at the head. They proceeded there immediately 2 platoons were sent forward to reinforce the strong post Huaggons Post and the remaining 2 platoons were kept at Batt HQ. They worked during the night connecting BIRD LONG & LA NEST with a communication trench.	
			When first 2 platoons of the 8th Queens arrived they were first quartered in the Brewery opposite HQ from whence they proceeded to take over posts evacuated by R Coy.	
			When the remainder of the 8th Queens arrived they were sent to take up a position lying in parallel to the Tempsile Road in front of the	
		9 pm	village which they did, about 9.0 pm.	

WAR DIARY
or
INTELLIGENCE SUMMARY.
(Erase heading not required.)

Army Form C. 2118.

Instructions regarding War Diaries and Intelligence Summaries are contained in F. S. Regs., Part II. and the Staff Manual respectively. Title pages will be prepared in manuscript.

Place	Date	Hour	Summary of Events and Information	Remarks and references to Appendices
In the field	30/11/17	9 p.m	Nice disabilities were ventilated until dawn. During the night the enemy shell transport parties & the like. We went out which endeavoured to the deliverer to Coy & in intention to note that 7/0 35007 R.M. Roberts N.C. with a few of the return party were able to reach Cater Copse & the cover positions of Stab Bank from which they stopes 16 bicycles two was done without interruption by the enemy.	

15/12/17

J M New
Lieut Col Comdg
19 Machine Gun Corps Inf

Vol 32

War "Diary
of the
1/9th Liverpool R.
for the period
1st to 31st December 1917.

Army Form C. 2118.

WAR DIARY
or
INTELLIGENCE SUMMARY.

(Erase heading not required.)

Instructions regarding War Diaries and Intelligence Summaries are contained in F. S. Regs., Part II. and the Staff Manual respectively. Title pages will be prepared in manuscript.

Place	Date	Hour	Summary of Events and Information	Remarks and references to Appendices
LEMPIRE	1/12/17	5 am	At morning "Stand to" today the position of affairs was as follows:- I was in command of the LEMPIRE sector. F15 C.1 &.2 The village was divided on the north by 2 Companies of 2nd Battalion who were occupying the trenches they had dug on 30 & Nov 17. On the north east it was defended by 2 Coy of the 8th Queens who had dug in on the approach line from F10.c.9.05 to F10.c.50.70. Base Bolagne north base bolagne built Renyeri West Orchard. But were held by the 8 Queens who also garrisoned YPK Zebra, Rougeir and BHQ. A section of the RE Field Coy. A party of 2 officers and about 100 Other Ranks worked who had been attached to the Burrelling Coy. During the morning the situation in LEMPIRE was fairly quiet. Enemy aircraft displayed considerable activity in low flying over the sector.	

C.B.Mercer Capt.

Army Form C. 2118.

Instructions regarding War Diaries and Intelligence Summaries are contained in F. S. Regs., Part II. and the Staff Manual respectively. Title pages will be prepared in manuscript.

WAR DIARY
or
INTELLIGENCE SUMMARY.
(Erase heading not required.)

Place	Date	Hour	Summary of Events and Information	Remarks and references to Appendices
LEMPIRE	1/12/17		The village was lightly shelled with trespire Gas shells several of which fell near Battalion HQ which necessitated the wearing of Respirators. From the vicinity of Battalion HQ it was possible to see the counter attack which was launched by Benger Lancers against the enemy who was holding VADRE POST and HOLT'S BANK. This counter attack seemed to be successful as the enemy were seen to depart expeditiously from their positions and Battalion observers reported that the cavalry were digging in somewhere near OSSUS I. From later accounts it appears that the Cavalry had to withdraw	
		9.30 pm	at night from the positions they had acquired. About 9-30 pm orders were received that the 9th Kings (Liverpool Regt) T.F. was to relieve the 6th Battalion of the same Regiment before dawn on the 2nd. Steps were taken to ascertain what posts were held by that Battalion & in what strength. These were :—	
			BIRD LANE 14 Other Ranks HEYTHROP LANE 20 Other Ranks	
			HEYTHROP POST 45 " " CRUCIFORM POST 45 " "	

D. D. & L., London, E.C.
(A 983) Wt. W6ojM1672 350,000 4/17 Sch. 82a Forms/C/2118/14

C B Turner Capt.

Army Form C. 2118.

WAR DIARY
or
INTELLIGENCE SUMMARY.
(Erase heading not required.)

Place	Date	Hour	Summary of Events and Information	Remarks and references to Appendices
LEMIRE	1/12/17		CATELET COPSE 11 Otherranks	
			PRIEL CUTTING 1 Company	
			THE NEST (Pt. Central) 1 Company	
			Machine guns were at the far end of PRIEL Cutting enfilading	
			the CATELET VALLEY, at Cruciform Post enfilading forty Pant.	
			The defence scheme was that the posts were to hold out	
			at all costs, and that if they were driven out to Headquarters	
			Company could man the bank at Battalion HQ, and if necessary,	
			a left defensive flank could be formed along the new trench which	
			had been dug extending BIRD LANE to Pit Central.	
2/12/17	6.10 a.m.	After resting as much as possible during the night the remaining	
			2 Companies of the 9th Battalion relieved the 6 Battalion and	
			relief was complete by 6.10 a.m.	
"	6.45 a.m.	About 6.45 am the enemy put down a heavy barrage covering	
			HEYTHROP & CRUCIFORM POSTS and the vicinity of Battalion HQ which	
			last for 3 quarters of an hour. No infantry attack followed.	

C.B. Brinner Capt.

Army Form C. 2118.

WAR DIARY
or
INTELLIGENCE SUMMARY.
(Erase heading not required.)

Instructions regarding War Diaries and Intelligence Summaries are contained in F. S. Regs., Part II. and the Staff Manual respectively. Title pages will be prepared in manuscript.

Place	Date	Hour	Summary of Events and Information	Remarks and references to Appendices
LEMPIRE	2/12/17		During the course of the morning the standing patrol in CATELET COPSE was driven back by a party of the enemy who were immediately evicted by a party of our bombers. It was reported that the enemy had placed a number of m. gunners in positions between KILDARE POST and DODOS HOP and he had a machine gun which enfiladed LEMPIRE ROAD in the neighbourhood of Batt HQ from KILDARE POST. On the whole the day was fairly quiet. At evening "stand to" the enemy again put down a barrage in its usual places as in the morning. After nightfall the following tasks were proceeded with:- 1. Deepening extension of Bird Lane to Battalion HQ. 2. New trench from Bird Lane to Keythrop Post. 3. New trench from Keythrop Post to Cruciform Post. 4. Wiring from Bird Lane to Keythrop Post from Keythrop Post to Cruciform Post & North of Priel Cutting. 5. C.T. from Battalion HQ towards LEMPIRE.	

WAR DIARY
or
INTELLIGENCE SUMMARY.
(Erase heading not required.)

Army Form C. 2118.

Instructions regarding War Diaries and Intelligence Summaries are contained in F. S. Regs., Part II. and the Staff Manual respectively. Title pages will be prepared in manuscript.

Place	Date	Hour	Summary of Events and Information	Remarks and references to Appendices
LEMPIRE	2/12/17		The night of 2/3/12 was passed in tranquility.	
	3/12/17		It was noticed that at morning "Stand to" the enemy's shell fire was considerably less. The enemy afterwards bombed the Standing Patrol at CATELET COPSE but he was driven back and	
		10.30 a.m.	the two re-established itself there about 10.30 a.m. The enemy shewed to battalion area at intervals and reports say his exploding fire along the Lempire Road. After nightfall he used Minenwerfen against the LEMPIRE ROAD and the vicinity of the posts. He attempted to prevent night was continued with the addition of the wiring of CATELET COPSE.	
			The night was fairly quiet.	
	3/4/17		During the night of Dec 3/4-17 the post at CATELET Copse heard cries coming from No Man's Land and an N.C.O. as it came light a native was seen lying in No Man's Land about half way between our trench and the enemy. The Officer in charge of the post at CATELET COPSE — 2nd Lieut A.O Ward MC — crawled out and though fired	

C B Smith Capt.

Army Form C. 2118.

WAR DIARY
or
INTELLIGENCE SUMMARY.
(Erase heading not required.)

Army Form C. 2118.

Place	Date	Hour	Summary of Events and Information	Remarks and references to Appendices
LEMPIRE	3/4/17		On 1/4 enemy Machine Guns succeeded in harassing the wounded man etc. He was found to be a Sergeant Major in the Bengal Lancers.	
	4/4/17		During the day the enemy was very quiet, the vicinity of PRIEL BANK was lightly shelled. The Machine Gun which was the previous day was very active from KILDARE Post was very quiet. He went on to trench joining up Crucifix to Keythrop and Grafton Posts who continued and the front wired. The road in the CT to Lempire was also continued. Patrols were sent out from Keythrop between Priel Bank but no enemy activity was observed.	
	5/4/17	7 am	At 7 am and 8 am our artillery shelled the enemy trenches at Kildare posn. Holts' Bank and the Birdcage. Several direct hits were observed. The retaliation from the enemy was very little, the principal targets being PRIEL FARM, No 13 Copse, Keythrop and Crucifix Posts. The remainder of the day was very quiet. At 12 noon the Commanding Officer of the	

Army Form C. 2118.

WAR DIARY
or
INTELLIGENCE SUMMARY.
(Erase heading not required.)

Instructions regarding War Diaries and Intelligence Summaries are contained in F. S. Regs., Part II. and the Staff Manual respectively. Title pages will be prepared in manuscript.

Place	Date	Hour	Summary of Events and Information	Remarks and references to Appendices
LEMPIRE	5/12/17	12 Noon	Dublin Fusiliers came to look over the Battalion area prior to taking over from me. At 12.30 p.m. I was informed that the Battalion would be relieved that night. The Dublin Fusiliers began to arrive about 5 p.m. and relief was complete by 9.30 p.m. Patrols were sent out to cover the relief. On relief the battalion proceeded to huts at St Emilie arriving there about 12.15 am. During the trip the casualties were 2 killed & 26 wounded.	
St EMELIE	6/12/17		The Battalion moved from this area about midday were conveyed by Motor Lorries to Billets in PERONNE. Here we stayed	
PERONNE	6/12/17		for 3 days, the battalion meanwhile cleaning up etc. While the Battalion were here all officers & men who were at the Reinforcement depot returned to us, which numbered 2 Officers & 30 other ranks. 2/L Anderson, H.R. and 2/L Sutherland J.P. being the officers. By the 8th inst the Battalion received orders for a further move & on the 10th inst the	
PERONNE	8/12/17		Battalion entrained at PERONNE Station about midday about 8 pm	

C.B. [illegible] Capt.

Army Form C. 2118.

WAR DIARY
or
INTELLIGENCE SUMMARY.
(Erase heading not required.)

19th Batt "The Kings" (Liverpool)

Instructions regarding War Diaries and Intelligence Summaries are contained in F.S. Regs., Part II. and the Staff Manual respectively. Title pages will be prepared in manuscript.

Place	Date	Hour	Summary of Events and Information	Remarks and references to Appendices
MOREUIL	10/9/17	8 pm	The battalion detrained at MOREUIL & marched to a camp just on the outskirts. The transport arrived here on the 11th inst after having a rather unpleasant trek owing to the weather not being very good. While the battalion remained here 1 officer & 2 other ranks arrived from the base. the officer being 2/Lt Manders &. On the morning of the 12th about 9.0 am	
BAILLVIE	12/9/17	9a	the battalion moved by route march to BAILLVIE. The transport followed in rear of the battalion.	
EPS.	13/9/17		On the 13th inst the battalion again moved by route march to EPS arriving there about 4.30 pm. the transport again following in rear of the battalion. When we arrived here Major Mace & Captain Glover rejoined from leave.	

E.J.Johnson
Capt.

Army Form C. 2118.

WAR DIARY
or
INTELLIGENCE SUMMARY.
(Erase heading not required.)

1/9 Batt "The Kings" (Liverpool Regt)

Instructions regarding War Diaries and Intelligence Summaries are contained in F. S. Regs., Part II. and the Staff Manual respectively. Title pages will be prepared in manuscript.

Place	Date	Hour	Summary of Events and Information	Remarks and references to Appendices
LISBOURG	15/9/17		On the 15th inst the Battalion moved by route march to its training area & occupied billets in LISBOURG	
	16/9/17		The 16th was spent by the Battalion in cleaning themselves up thoroughly. Also on this date 2 officers reported for duty they being 2/Lt Andrews C.A. & 2/Lt Prior E.J.	
	17/9/17		On the 17th the Battalion had the Divisional Baths allotted to them. The following improvements were carried out by the Battalion in the training area. (1) A miniature range was constructed to accommodate 30 men firing at once (2) A Lewis gun range was constructed to accommodate 4 Lewis Guns firing at once. This range contains 12 targets length of range 100 and 200 yds. (3) Bayonet fighting course was constructed which includes 3 trenches and 3 sets of pieceaus (4) Les attornesing Trenches were dug and (5) A Aid was erected by the training area by the Regimental Pioneers and in this area	

G.H. Monroe
Capt.

Army Form C. 2118.

WAR DIARY
or
INTELLIGENCE SUMMARY.

(Erase heading not required.)

Instructions regarding War Diaries and Intelligence Summaries are contained in F. S. Regs., Part II. and the Staff Manual respectively. Title pages will be prepared in manuscript.

14 Kings (Coy) April

Place	Date	Hour	Summary of Events and Information	Remarks and references to Appendices
LISBOURG			Units of every description are made. Training which includes the following is carried out each day:- Close order drill; Handling of Arms; Bayonet fighting; Rapid Wiring. Physical training; Musketry which includes firing on ranges practice in rapid loading, Triangle of error; Trigger pressing etc. Every day the Young Officers of the battalion are receiving instruction in the Lewis Gun & in the evening they also are given lectures or demonstrations. Training of Signallers is also carried out.	
LISBOURG	23		The Battalion had a route march today the distance covered being 8½ miles. The Officers reported for duty with the Battalion today. 2/Lt Halewood.	
"	24		The Battalion concert party gave an entertainment today which was very well appreciated.	

Army Form C.2118.

WAR DIARY
or
INTELLIGENCE SUMMARY.
(Erase heading not required.)

1/9 The King's (Liverpool Regt)

Place	Date	Hour	Summary of Events and Information	Remarks and references to Appendices
LISBOURG	25/12/17		This being Christmas day the battalion were excused all parades with the exception of Rifle inspections. At 2.0.p.m Christmas Dinner was served to each Company which was greatly appreciated.	
	31/12/17		Capt Leath RN(RAMC) reported to take over duties as M.O. from Capt Harrison M.B. who unfortunately had to return to 13rd West Lancs Fd Amb on account of ill health.	

Rec/d 2/1/18

F M Few
Lieut-Col Comdg
1/9th Bn "The King's" (Liverpool Regiment)

WAR DIARY or INTELLIGENCE SUMMARY.

Army Form C. 2118.

The Kings (Liverpool Regiment) 1st Battalion.

Place	Date	Hour	Summary of Events and Information	Remarks and references to Appendices
LISBOURG	Jany 19/1/16		On the 19th of the Month the Batln were again attached to the Battalion. The next few days the Battalion carried on with its usual training, which also included firing on ranges etc. The signallers carried on with their own programme of training.	
"	8/1/16		On the 8th inst there was an Inter Coy evening Competition held and although the weather was very cold some very good work was done. "A" Coy proved themselves to be the Best Coy in the Competition. During the next few days the usual training including firing on ranges etc. and carried out. On the 23rd inst a Staff Sergt Major from the Army Gymnastic School reported for duty. During his stay his work consisted chiefly in training the junior N.C.O's in Physical Drill and Bayonet fighting. He also took the Companies over the Assault Course. By the 24/1/16 the Battalion went en route march, about 10 miles. On the 25th inst Lieut Colonel Reid received a private letter from the Major General Commanding the 55th Division intimating that a Change was about to take place which would	
	23/1/16			
	24/1/16			

WAR DIARY
or
INTELLIGENCE SUMMARY.

Army Form C. 2118.

1/9 Battalion The King's (Liverpool Regt.) T.F.

Place	Date	Hour	Summary of Events and Information	Remarks and references to Appendices
LISBOURG	26/1/18		About every Division in the British Armies in so much that Brigades would only be composed of 3 Battalions instead of 4. Unfortunately from information received from G.H.Q. the Major General reported that this Battalion would have to leave the 165 Infy Brigade, and would in all probability with the 2nd line Battalion	
	27/1/18		On the 27th inst we received orders confirmation of the above, from the 55th Division. We also intimated that we should be required to this only 12 Officers and 200 Other Ranks along to the 2nd line. On the 28th inst a letter was received informing us that 3 drafts would have to be found, which would consist of the following:— 12th Kings — — — 5 Officers 100 Other Ranks / 1st Kings — — — 10 Officers 200 Other Ranks / 4th Kings — — — 10 Officers 200 Other Ranks	
	29/1/18		The draft for the 12th Kings had to proceed by Lorries on the 29th inst. As we could not supply the full number of men asked for	

Army Form C. 2118.

WAR DIARY
or
INTELLIGENCE SUMMARY.

(Erase heading not required.)

Army Form C. 2118.

1/9 Battalion The King's (Liverpool Regiment) T.F.

Place	Date	Hour	Summary of Events and Information	Remarks and references to Appendices
LISBOURG			As the two drafts of men were posted to the Battalion in equal proportions, the 'draft' to the 1/5 Kings left on the 29th inst & consisted of 5 Officers and 80 Other Ranks. The remainder carried on a route march, about 8 miles. On the 30th inst. two drafts for the 1/12 & 1/7 Kings left for their respective units. The strength of these drafts were 1/12 Kings - 10 Officers and 192 Other Ranks: 1/7 Kings - 10 Officers and 189 Other Ranks. These drafts left all ranks were nearly affected, as the majority of them had fought together in a platoon during the past 3 years. The Divisional Concert Party came along to LISBOURG on the 30th & gave a very good Concert, which was enjoyed by everyone who was lucky enough to be present. On the 31st inst. the remainder of the Battalion eventually left for the 57th Division to join the 2/9th Bn. There were 8 Officers & 15th Other Ranks. Activities left LISBOURG, the remainder being either on leave or on courses. Everyone paraded in the square at LISBOURG and at 10.30 am the Major General	

2353 Wt. W2544/1454 700,000 5/15 D. D. & L. A.D.S.S./Forms/C. 2118.

WAR DIARY or INTELLIGENCE SUMMARY

Army Form C. 2118.

(Erase heading not required)

Regiment/Battalion: 9th Battalion "The King's" (Liverpool Regt.) T.F.

Instructions regarding War Diaries and Intelligence Summaries are contained in F.S. Regs., Part II. and the Staff Manual respectively. Title pages will be prepared in manuscript.

Place	Date	Hour	Summary of Events and Information	Remarks and references to Appendices
LISBURNE	31/7/15	10/30 a.m.	Visited us and made a farewell speech. In this speech he gave a glowing tribute to the Battalion, dealing with the fine work done by them during the 2 years they have been together. There were also present the Brigadier General, Brigade Major & representatives from the 5th, 6th & 7th King's to give the Battalion a good send off. The [crossed out] bands from the 5th & 7th King's were also present & rendered selections. As the Battalion eventually moved off in lorries, the bands of the 7th King's played "Auld Lang Syne". Great notification was also received from O.C. that the Commanding Officer of the 9th Bn The King's (amalgamated 1st & 2nd Line B.n's) would be Lieut Colonel J.W.M. DREW D.S.O. 2nd L. R.E. Captain (A/Major) R.E. BURNETT 2nd in Command. Lieut [?] Quartermaster of the 9th Bn acting also appointed Quartermaster.	

F M Drew Lt Col

Army Form C. 2118.

WAR DIARY
or
INTELLIGENCE SUMMARY.
(Erase heading not required.)

Instructions regarding War Diaries and Intelligence Summaries are contained in F. S. Regs., Part II. and the Staff Manual respectively. Title pages will be prepared in manuscript.

Place	Date	Hour	Summary of Events and Information	Remarks and references to Appendices
VECKE	1.2.19		Coy parade for inspection. Education	
"	2.2.19		Divine Service for all denominations	
"	3.2.19	15.00	Bn. parade for inspection. Recreational Training & Education	
"	4.2.19		Battalion parade for route march. Education	
"	5.2.19		Reorganisation of coys. under 3 coy org.	
"	6.2.19		"	
"	7.2.19		Battalion parade for inspection. Education	
"	8.2.19		Battalion training	
"	9.2.19		Divine Services for all denominations	
"	10.2.19		Battalion parade for inspection. Recreational Training	
"	11.2.19		Battalion parade for inspection. Recreational Training & Education	
"	12.2.19		Battalion parade for musketry. Rifle inspection by C.O.	
"	13.2.19		Battalion parade for inspection. Recreational Training	
"	14.2.19		Coy parade under coy. for fatigues & Recreational Training	
"	15.2.19		Battalion parade for inspection. Recreational Training	
"	16.2.19		Divine Services for all denominations	

Lieut Colonel
Commanding 1/8th (Rifle) Bn., "The King's"
(L'pool Regt.)

WAR DIARY
or
INTELLIGENCE SUMMARY.

(Erase heading not required.)

Army Form C. 2118.

Instructions regarding War Diaries and Intelligence Summaries are contained in F. S. Regs., Part II. and the Staff Manual respectively. Title pages will be prepared in manuscript.

Place	Date	Hour	Summary of Events and Information	Remarks and references to Appendices
Decles	17.2.19		Company trainers for instruction. Arrive of Brigade from	
"	18.2.19		rejoined the Bn. from Leave. Divine Service. Company of the Bn. Company training. Baths. Parade. Semi-Final Training	
"	19.2.19		Continued preparation for instruction. Bn disintegration Army	
"	20.2.19		Company rendezvous at forest.	
"	21.2.19		Company parades for instruction. Arm drill, inspections, etc.	
"	22.2.19		Continued parade for instruction. Armouries inspections etc	
"	23.2.19		Divine Service for all denominations.	
"	24.2.19		Company trainers. Armourial investing Farrier.	
"	25.2.19		Company inspection. checkout of the Armoury.	
"	26.2.19		Battalion Baths.	
"	27.2.19		Company Invals. Company drill, etc etc. Farriery	
"	28.2.19		Company training. Cmdy drill inspections Farriery	

J. M. Kay
Lieut Colonel
Commanding 1/8th (Rifle) Bn., "The King's"
(L'Pool Regt.)

www.ingramcontent.com/pod-product-compliance
Lightning Source LLC
Chambersburg PA
CBHW081356160426
43192CB00013B/2422